the **smart approach to**®

kids'
ROOMS

Third Edition

girls rule!

CREATIVE
HOMEOWNER®

the smart approach to ®
kids'
ROOMS

Third Edition

Megan Connelly

CREATIVE HOMEOWNER®, Upper Saddle River, New Jersey

THE SMART APPROACH TO® KIDS' ROOMS, THIRD EDITION

SENIOR EDITOR	Kathie Robitz
EDITOR	Lisa Kahn
SENIOR GRAPHIC DESIGN COORDINATOR	Glee Barre
PHOTO RESEARCHER	Robyn Poplasky
EDITORIAL ASSISTANTS	Jennifer Calvert and Nora Grace
INDEXER	Schroeder Indexing Services
DIGITAL IMAGING SPECIALIST	Frank Dyer
COVER DESIGN	Glee Barre
FRONT COVER PHOTOGRAPHY	Mark Lohman
INSIDE FRONT COVER PHOTOGRAPHY	(both) Tony Giammarino/Giammarino & Dworkin
BACK COVER PHOTOGRAPHY	(top left) Greg Hursley; (top right) Beth Singer; (bottom) Tria Giovan
INSIDE BACK COVER PHOTOGRAPHY	(top) Tony Giammarino/Giammarino & Dworkin, (bottom) Bob Greenspan, Stylist: Susan Andrews

CREATIVE HOMEOWNER

VICE PRESIDENT AND PUBLISHER	Timothy O. Bakke
PRODUCTION DIRECTOR	Kimberly H. Vivas
ART DIRECTOR	David Geer
MANAGING EDITOR	Fran J. Donegan

Current Printing (last digit)
10 9 8 7 6 5 4 3 2

The Smart Approach to® Kids' Rooms, Third Edition
Library of Congress Control Number: 2007933858
ISBN10: 1-58011-389-3
ISBN-13: 978-1-58011-389-2

CREATIVE HOMEOWNER®
A Division of Federal Marketing Corp.
24 Park Way
Upper Saddle River, NJ 07458
www.creativehomeowner.com

dedication

For my beautiful children, Sheila and Aedan,
and their wonderful father, Joe.

acknowledgments

The completion of this book would hardly have been possible without the encouragement, support, and patience of my editor, Kathie Robitz. In this, as in all things, she is one of a kind. Thank you, too, to Lisa Kahn and Glee Barre of Creative Homeowner, whose talents for editing and designing keep this project up-to-the-minute. In addition, I would also like to thank the following resources: The Juvenile Products Manufacturers Association, The Consumer Product Safety Commission, The Allergy and Asthma Network of Fairfax, Virginia, and the countless parents of children with special needs who have taken to the Internet to share their experiences and innovative ideas for enhancing the lives of their children.

contents

introduction

Bending over to tuck the blanket into the crib, your excitement builds as you add the last few touches to the nursery you have decorated for your soon-to-arrive bundle of joy. Along with your anticipation, you hope that everything is safe, secure, and just right for the baby to be. As you glance around the room, you might question whether you should have chosen soothing pastel colors instead of stimulating primaries. You needn't worry; someday that tiny child will have no trouble telling you exactly what she likes. The colors you select now might someday seem too babyish to a child who is taking her first steps toward independence.

Children grow up too fast. Just when you become comfortable with one phase, they suddenly mature and their tastes—and requirements— change. No problem. *The Smart Approach to® Kids' Rooms, Third Edition* can help you. On these pages, you will see how to work with space, choose appropriate color combinations, and shop for furniture, flooring, and window treatments while sticking to a budget.

10

Looking for creative ideas for projects you can do yourself? You'll find all of the inspiration you need, plus a few do-it-yourself tips, to add personality to the room with paint, wallcovering, or fabric.

Chapter 1, "A Place To Start" (pages 12–31), gives you the inside edge on planning space. If you've ever wondered how professional designers manage to bring together all of the elements in a room so that they always look perfectly in place, you'll find the answers here. This chapter will help you to understand and apply basic design concepts to creating your child's room. You'll learn how to properly measure the space so that you can develop a floor plan on paper. There's also advice

for creating a budget and how to anticipate professional fees.

Chapter 2, "The Magic of Color" (pages 32–49), features plenty of ideas that will help you develop a palette and mix patterns and prints pleasingly.

Chapter 3, "Great Furniture" (pages 50–75), contains some of the most important information in the book—how to shop for a bed and mattress. You'll also find practical guidance for furnishing the room and creating storage with style.

Chapter 4, "Walls, Windows & Floors" (pages 76–99), tells you all you need to know about paint and wallpaper, including how

to estimate quantities, and details choices for window treatments and flooring materials.

Chapter 5, "Decorating the Nursery" (pages 100–117), addresses the specific needs of a newborn's room, from choosing a crib to creating a design theme. This chapter also includes an important checklist to help you safeguard the nursery.

Chapter 6, "Designs Toddlers Will Love" (118–137), discusses the transition from baby nursery to child's bedroom. You'll find helpful, safety-minded hints for furnishing and decorating a room suitable for a toddler's expanding world. This means creating areas for play as well as sleep.

Chapter 7, "Expanding Young Horizons" (pages 138–157), presents a host of ideas for rooms designed with young, school-age children in mind. It's chock full of furniture and storage solutions that will delight parents and kids alike.

Chapter 8, "Stylish Teen Havens" (pages 158–179), may hold the answer to waste management in some households. You may never need to keep the door shut again.

Chapter 9, "Special Needs" (pages 180–191), offers a starting point for designing a room for a child with various physical challenges or medical issues. In this chapter, you find that "special" is synonymous with "stylish."

Chapter 10, "Bathrooms for Kids" (pages 192–201), is a portfolio of terrific kids' baths that's accompanied by important advice about safety.

The Appendix (pages 202–207) provides handy furniture templates and a grid that you can copy for working out a floor plan on paper.

Consult the Resource Guide (pages 208–211) for industry-related manufacturers and associations, and see the glossary for a helpful list of terms and definitions.

Most of all—have fun!

1

a place to start

Because so much of the family's attention is focused on the needs of a newborn, it seems like everyone practically lives in the baby's room. But as time goes on, a child's room becomes a place apart from other family spaces. Decorating the bedroom of a very young child is fun because it gives parents a chance to re-create some of their own childhood fantasies. As children grow and develop preferences, they can help Mom and Dad make decisions about furniture, colors, and themes. But don't run off to the paint store yet. It pays to plan ahead of time how much work will be involved and what you will be able to spend. Your goal should be a room that suits your son's or daughter's individuality and that is attractive, comfortable, and flexible enough to grow with your child. That way, you won't have to redecorate for many years to come.

LEFT
Whimsical details and warm, inviting hues combine to make this bedroom the perfect spot for sweet dreams.

I n this chapter, you'll learn how to develop a plan of action that will help you assess your existing space and explore ideas for making improvements. Follow the easy steps on pages 16–17 to help with this process.

After you've made your analysis, you'll be able to compile a list of things you want to achieve with the new design—and decide whom you want to do the work. If you're thinking of doing the work yourself, first take the quiz on page 16 to determine whether this is a reasonable solution.

It's wise to put together a realistic budget for a project in advance so that you don't run out of money midway through the renovation. If you're all thumbs when it comes to hammering out figures, follow the advice that begins on page 24.

ABOVE
Look for dual-purpose design elements. This window seat provides a cozy niche for reading and doubles as a two-drawer storage box for clothes or toys.

LEFT
An unusual chandelier, painted to coordinate with the pretty furnishings, makes a delightful accent piece while functioning as an ambient light source.

evaluating
the space

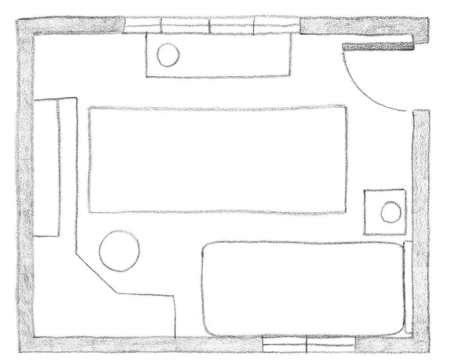

More than anything else, rely on your own taste and intuition, and that of your child's, because there are no hard and fast rules for decorating. However, it always helps to keep in mind the basic principles of scale, proportion, line, balance, harmony, and rhythm when examining space—and all of the ways to fill it up. This is what professional designers do to create interiors that are both pleasing to the eye and practical for living. To get acquainted with these concepts, consult the Smart Tip box, "Design Basics," on page 19.

It's an excellent idea to put your thoughts on paper. So with notepad and pencil in hand, take a walk around the room at various times of the day. Is the room too small or too large? Are the furnishings the proper scale for the space? Is it easy or difficult to arrange furniture in the room? How many doors and windows are there? Are they conveniently placed? Is the room too dark or too bright at certain times of the day? Are there enough closets and other types of storage space? You may have to live with some or all of the physical drawbacks of the space, but recognizing them will inspire you to find ways to change them or work around them.

Next, look at the condition of the surfaces. Do the walls simply need repainting or new wallpaper, or is there damage that requires repair? Kids can also be pretty tough on floors and carpeting. Take stock of the existing furniture. Is it adequate for your child's needs? What condition is it in? Minor damage to the finish, missing knobs, and drawers that stick or need re-gluing are all easy repair jobs. Don't forget to get input from the person who occupies the room, too. Her perception of the space is the most important aspect of your analysis.

Your notes will help you focus on what can stay and what must go. Then, you'll be able to organize your analysis into an action plan.

ABOVE
To determine what fits where, draw a floor plan that includes window and door openings; then rough-in the furnishings.

LEFT
Showing your child a more detailed floor plan that includes the color scheme and specific objects will help you include her in the process.

smart steps
your action plan

■ Step 1   MEASURE UP

Use a steel measuring tape to figure the overall dimensions of the room. Include the size of all of the openings (doors and windows). If there are any fixed features, such as a built-in desk or bookcases, measure and record their sizes, too.

Measure the existing furniture. With just a few adjustments to the layout, you may save yourself the expense of buying something new. If you're planning shelf storage for bulky items such as electronic equipment, measure the components.

Make a freehand sketch of the space and the furnishings, recording the measurements you've taken in the margin. Don't forget to note the electrical switches and outlets, cable and phone jacks, radiators, heat registers, air ducts, and light fixtures.

■ Step 2   DRAW A FLOOR PLAN TO SCALE

This will be an invaluable reference when you're shopping for furniture or arranging the layout of the room. Consult the Appendix, which shows the standard symbols used to indicate permanent features on your plan. Use shorthand; for example, for 3 feet and 2 inches, write 3' 2". Work on $\frac{1}{4}$-inch graph paper. Each square will represent one foot. For example, if a wall measures 15 feet, the line you draw for that wall will use 15 squares. Use a ruler or straightedge to make your lines; then record your measurements.

To experiment with different furniture arrangements, first draw and cut out furniture templates, using the same $\frac{1}{4}$-inch scale. Then, refer to the standard furniture symbols in the Appendix. While each one is drawn to scale based on average dimensions, you'll have to adjust the scale to your furniture's actual size. If you plan to buy new pieces, ask the salesperson to give you the manufacturer's spec sheets, which will include dimensions. It's never a good idea to guess the size of a large piece of furniture.

■ Step 3   CREATE A FOCAL POINT

When you're playing with the room's layout and furniture arrangement, start by placing the largest piece first; this is typically the bed—the room's focal point. The focal point is the first element that grabs your attention when you walk into the room. Even if it's a simple twin-size bed, where you locate it and how you dress it makes an impact on your overall design.

should you do it yourself?

Answer these questions honestly; then judge for yourself.

■ How extensive is the project? If you're just giving the room a facelift, you can probably handle the job. But if something requires a special skill, such as electrical work or building bookshelves, leave it to a professional.

■ Do you have enough spare time to commit to the project? Painting the walls may take a weekend; overhauling the entire space and ordering and assembling furniture can take weeks.

■ Are you patient and persistent? Can you follow through to the end? Don't start anything you can't finish.

■ Do you enjoy physical work, such as removing and hanging wallpaper, installing flooring material, or refinishing furniture?

■ Have you ever done this type of work before?

■ Do you know what tools are required for specific jobs? Do you own them?

■ Will you need assistance? If a task requires more than two hands, can you get the help you need when you need it?

■ Do you have the confidence to make all of the decorating decisions yourself? If you hit a snag, are you willing to call in a consultant, such as a professional interior designer? Is there any room in your budget to cover the cost of bringing in a professional if you make a mistake you can't fix yourself?

Clearances. Whenever possible, plan enough space around the furniture for comfortable use. For example, if there will be under-bed storage, such as roll-out drawers, make sure there's enough room on the side of the bed to fully access them. Although you're limited by the actual size of the room, professionals recommend the following minimum allowances, whenever possible:

- 22 inches of space around the bed
- 36 inches of space between the bed and any door that opens into the bedroom
- 18 inches between two beds for a small table and a pathway
- 36 inches of space in front of a closet for dressing and sorting items of clothing
- 40 inches of space into the room to open dresser drawers
- 10 to 20 inches of space to sit comfortably in a chair at a desk, plus 12 to 16 more inches to pull back the chair and rise from it
- a distance that is three times the size of the TV screen for optimal viewing

TOP LEFT AND RIGHT
The window seat, shelves, and desk in this room are designed to coordinate. You can paint furniture a single color to make mismatched pieces work together.

BOTTOM
The bed here takes its color cue from other furniture in the room and becomes part of a cohesive scheme.

Take note of the location of vents, heating or air-conditioning units, phone jacks, and electrical switches and outlets. Maintain a distance of 6 inches between baseboard heating and air-conditioning units and furniture. Don't obstruct electrical outlets or switches.

Traffic Patterns. Make traffic patterns as convenient as possible for you and your children. For example, in a nursery, locate the changing table closest to the door and the crib farther into the room.

Traffic patterns are especially important in shared rooms. Allow clearances for one child to pass another child without disruption when someone is seated at a desk or playing on the floor. Strategic storage in the play area will be used more often than something that's inconvenient. If your kids play in the middle of the floor, a rolling cart that can be pushed against the wall when not in use can make picking up toys less of a chore.

Adaptability. Floor plans that include present and future needs can help when you're making decisions about furniture. If you're planning to stay in the same house, consider how the room you design now can be adapted later as your child grows older and requires more furniture and storage.

shared spaces

Common areas and equally important private ones are necessary to preserve the peace in a room shared by two children. Size isn't as important as organized function paired with an understanding of the unique personalities and needs of the two kids who will use the room.

When those two children are very young, a shared play area can totally dominate the space. That means you'll have to find a way to partially block off the sleeping area so that one child can rest quietly while the other plays, if necessary. Doubled storage space for toys helps to promote shared responsibility. Each child should be expected to care for her own things.

School-age kids require separate quiet places for reading, studying, and hobby pursuits. Take into account the different study habits and interests of siblings when you're planning these places. As a child differentiates himself and develops his own interests, his need for private space, where he is totally in control, becomes more important for maturing with a healthy sense of self. Both children benefit from having clearly defined areas where the other child cannot play or use things without asking his roommate first.

The problems become a bit more difficult when children who are separated by several years share space. Younger children don't understand property rights as of yet. In these situations, walls or half-walls make sharing a room easier.

Dividing Up the Space

Begin by listing the needs of each child. In most cases, kids can share some areas. Play space, the TV viewing area, and hobby tables can often accommodate overlapping needs. For older children, separate desks and computer equipment may have to be planned. A feature such as an aquarium or a special wall decoration should be equally available to both children, unless there is another agreement by both children and parents. Before you divide up the space in a room, involve the children in the planning process. Who gets what should be decided up front; that way everybody will be happy with the results.

Furniture Dividers. Modular furniture that incorporates individual pieces for sleeping, studying, and storage can be used effectively to divide space in a shared room. (See "Modular Systems," on page 58.) It allows for design flexibility in almost any layout and can be adapted to the age, tastes, hobbies, and habits of each child.

OPPOSITE
For school-age children, a quiet space for homework and projects is essential. A separate-but-equal arrangement in this room complements its spare design.

ABOVE
Bunk beds free floor space for other interests and necessary furniture. At bedtime, the arrangement gives children visual privacy from each other.

smart tip DESIGN BASICS

Professionals rely on the principles of scale and proportion, line, balance, harmony, and rhythm when designing a room. By applying these concepts, you'll be able to make the most of the room's best attributes and play down the less-appealing features of the space.

- Scale and proportion work hand in hand. Scale refers to an object's size as it relates to the size of everything else. Proportion refers to the relationship of objects to one another based on their size.
- Line defines and shapes space. Vertical lines appear strong; horizontal lines appear restful; diagonal lines express motion or transition; and curved lines denote softness.
- Balance refers to the even placement of things of varying sizes and shapes around the room. Balanced relationships can be either symmetrical or asymmetrical.
- Harmony is achieved when everything coordinates within a single scheme or motif.
- Rhythm refers to repeated forms. While harmony pulls a room together, rhythm or repetition of a pattern or shape moves your eye around it.

Tall, freestanding bookcases are another good idea for divvying up space in a room. Enclosed units can be used back-to-back or side by side. In the latter case, the backs can provide a surface for posters, or your children can use them as bulletin boards. If this arrangement blocks light, consider half-size bookcases or freestanding open shelving. Hang a fabric shade from the top of an open shelving unit. When privacy is desired, the shade can be rolled down.

Armoires and wardrobes are another solution. Place them back to back or stagger them to create a room divider.

Half Walls. A good way to delineate space is with a half wall. If your budget allows, hire a carpenter to construct one at wainscot level, 30 to 40 inches high. Half walls provide privacy for children while they're seated or lying in bed, and at the same time allow good light and air circulation throughout both sides of the room. Plus, you can build storage into the divider.

Modifying the Shape of a Room

Some rooms are just oddly shaped. Fortunately, you can disguise this imperfection, or draw attention away from it, with visual tricks. For example;

■ *If the room is long,* divide the space by creating two major groupings of furniture. One way is to make a sleeping space apart from the play and work zone. Use area rugs to anchor each group in the divided space. You can also use square shapes, such as area rugs, to "widen" the space.

■ *If the room is narrow,* arrange furniture on the diagonal. Place the bed catty-cornered. Again, introduce more squares into the room—cube-shaped chests or a large, square mirror, for example. Group pieces of artwork in a square-shaped arrangement on a prominent wall.

smart tip ROOM FOR TWO

Even when you can't physically divide a room, you can use a few visual tricks that will make both kids feel as if they've got their own private space.

- Position the heads of each bed so that the children are looking away from each other, not toward each other.
- Locate reading or task lighting so that it's confined to each child's area without spillover.
- Select a different color to identify each child's belongings. Use a common print or a third color to bridge the two. (See Chapter 2, "The Magic of Color," beginning on page 32, for more tips.)
- If both kids like the same color, go into reverse. For example, use white polka dots on a blue background for one child's bedding, blue polka dots on a white background for the other one. Many fabrics are available in reverse colorations.
- If one section of the room is cut off from natural light and there's no outside wall where you can add another window, consider a roof window or skylight to brighten the darker half of the space.
- Use mirrors to make small areas appear larger.

LEFT
Kids sharing a room must determine their priorities before picking furniture. The mini-gym in this room was possible because bunk beds were used to free up floor space.

TOP
Another way to free up space is by investing in well-organized closets. If closets are large enough, you can even fit furniture inside them, eliminating the need for bulky dressers.

OPPOSITE
Providing a place for everything is the first step in creating a neat room. Between the hanging storage and these pullout drawers, everything from clothing and shoes to toys is accommodated and neatly concealed behind closed doors.

■ *If the ceiling is low,* add height with tall furnishings, such as bookcases, a highboy dresser, or an armoire. You might also consider window treatments that extend above the window frame and hang from the area just below the ceiling to the floor. Use as many vertical lines in the room as possible, even on wall and fabric treatments. Vertical-striped wallpaper or curtains are good examples.

■ *If the ceiling is high,* lower the scale of the space by incorporating more horizontal lines in the room. Install molding one-half or three-quarters of the way up the walls to visually shorten them. Hang pictures lower on the wall.

Sometimes a room, particularly one built under attic eaves, has too many angles, which makes the space look chopped up. An easy way to camouflage this problem is by painting all of the surfaces, including the ceiling, a single color. Wallpaper featuring a small print will accomplish the same thing.

More Strategies for Success

Most parents confront a common problem when decorating their kids' rooms: lack of space. To complicate matters, kids have a lot of stuff, and they're pack rats. They will collect everything from stuffed animals to computer software (not to mention the plastic trinkets that come with fast-food meals), plus an assortment of other paraphernalia that finds its way into the room and never comes out. Before you attempt to provide a place for everything, remember: things will seldom be kept in their designated place, and more stuff is always on the way.

You can avoid a lot of the conflict that inevitably develops over messy rooms by setting aside a day—once a week, once a month, or at the beginning of each season, whatever suits you—to do an inventory with your child of what stays and what goes. Begin with the clothes. If it no longer fits or hasn't been worn in a while, get rid of it. Give the item to charity, hand it down, or toss it—just get it out of the room.

Next, hit the toys. Quietly pack off to the attic or basement whatever lies untouched for a while. When present favorites lose their appeal, stow them away and bring out the ones in storage. This rotation keeps clutter down. New toys simply replace current ones, which can be packed away with the others. Keep this process ongoing. School-age kids might balk, but reassure them that they may exchange any stored item for something that's in their room. Admittedly, the older the child, the harder it is to enforce this system. But it's worth a try. Sometimes they simply have to live with it.

School worksheets, tests, and artwork can quickly turn a room into a real mess if there's no place to organize them. A small metal file cabinet is an inexpensive solution, and it doesn't take up much space. You can spray-paint it to match the decor, or simply cover it with a pretty tablecloth and let it double as a nightstand. Create a large hanging file for papers from each school year. Oversized artwork can be stored in a flat art portfolio that can slip easily into a closet for safekeeping.

Even the smallest room can store things efficiently if you make the most out of every square inch. Plastic stacking bins, under-bed drawers and boxes, and shelving all help to keep stuff out of sight without much effort or added expenditure.

developing a budget

Before getting carried away with plans or ideas, devise a budget for the project. You may already know your bottom line: the total amount you can afford to spend. With that in mind, make a list of everything you'd like to buy for the room. Something you can't afford now may be a more realistic purchase six months from now. You don't have to make all of your changes right away. Take your shopping list with you, and make product and price comparisons. Note all of the style and item numbers, as well as the names of the colors and patterns. You'll need this information, especially for things you may put off

purchasing until later. When you've narrowed down your selections, create a worksheet, such as the one on the opposite page. It will show you where you stand, and it can serve as a permanent record for your files.

Professional Fees

What if you have to hire professional help? Sometimes, seeking the services of a professional is the most practical thing you can do to keep costs down. Whether it's for a design consultation or a contractor's fees, it often makes more sense to pay for someone's expertise rather than risk costly mistakes. Most professionals will gladly give you an estimate. Take that figure and pad it a bit—just to be on the safe side. You never know what problems may come up that can boost the original estimates of the job. Expect to pay more and you might come out ahead.

LEFT
A careful accounting of expenditures can help you to see where you might be able to cut costs. Finding a bit of extra cash in the budget might enable you to include something special, such as hiring a muralist.

OPPOSITE
With custom-built furniture, a professional designer can develop a plan that fits the unique contours of the room. Here, each child has a very private bunk and a window seat with storage all to himself.

Interior Designers. A professional designer's practiced eye can help you rearrange or reuse many of the things you already own. By offering suggestions for how you can refinish or relocate a piece of furniture, or where you can find great buys on secondhand stuff, she can save you lots of money in the long run. Even little tips about arranging wall art, eliminating clutter, using color effectively, or coordinating prints and fabrics are worth the relatively few dollars you'll spend for the advice. Many interior designers will consult for an hourly rate, which can be less than $100 in some cases. Larger projects are often negotiated for a flat fee. Don't be afraid to ask for design advice where you shop; sometimes, it's free.

Contractors. Tradespeople such as carpenters, painters, and wallpaper hangers typically work for an hourly rate, which varies across the country. When a contractor gives you an estimate, it's a compilation of how much time he thinks it will take to do the work, plus the cost of materials, such as paint. Get a few estimates (and at least three references) before hiring a contractor to perform any work for you.

RIGHT
A painted mural can create a fantasy world within the bedroom. Try an illustration from a favorite storybook or bring a beloved stuffed animal to life.

A SAMPLE BUDGET WORKSHEET

Item	Manufacturer/ Retailer	Style/ Pattern	Color	Immediate Purchase Costs	Future Purchase Costs
Furniture					
Bed	Slocum's	"Ashley"	Antique White	799	
Mattress Set	Slocum's	#0335	—	500	
Armoire	Slocum's	antique			1,200
Dresser	Slocum's	"Ashley"	Antique White	599	
Wall Treatments					
Paint	No Name	Premium	Blush	80	
Wallpaper	Home Center	My Toile	Rouge		160
Window Treatments					
Blinds	Home Center	Plantation	White	60	
Curtains	custom				500
Valance	Slocum's	Paisley	Pink	40	
Flooring					
Wall-to Wall					
Carpeting	Carpet City	$8/sq.ft.	Champagne		1,200
Area Rug	Slocum's	Posies	Pink	100	
Lighting					
Lamps	Slocum's	2 Candlestick	White	60	
Chandelier	antique	6-arm			250
Bedding					
Quilt	Slocum's	Pink Ribbons	Pink	75	
Duvet Set	custom				200
Accent Pillows	custom				50
Accessories					
Wall Art					150
Mirror	The Boutique	Wicker	White	50	
	—	—			
			TOTALS	**$2,363**	**$3,710**

LEFT
If you are artistically inclined, you can create a mural of your own design on your child's wall. For parents who are less handy with a paintbrush, many wallpaper manufacturers feature ready-made murals you can apply yourself.

design workbook
COORDINATION IS KEY

right on hue

The easiest way to pick a paint color is to pull one from the bedding, left, or window treatment fabrics. Paint and fabrics are inexpensive enough to replace later.

shine forth

Natural light can be enhanced by a minimal window treatment. Recessed lights provide ambient room lighting. Desk lamps provide task lighting.

throw a curve

To contrast the rectilinear shapes, a curvy design was chosen for the desk chair. Swirls and circles continue in the comforter pattern. (See also top left.)

both sides now

Achieve balance in a room by arranging objects symmetrically. Here, the built-in desk echoes the nightstand. (See also far left and left.)

design workbook
SPANNING THE YEARS

room to expand

If space is not at a premium, consider a full- or even queen-size bed for a child's room. It will come in handy if the room occasionally doubles as a guest room.

good wood

Solid furniture that doesn't appear juvenile remains suitable from tot to teen years. This set provides plenty of storage niches for the treasures and trinkets kids collect.

homework happens

Before you know it, a school-age kid needs his own desk, top, and computer space. Allot room for it, and plan for ample electrical outlets and lighting sources.

from disney to mtv

The details on this media unit, left, can be replaced as tastes change. Be sure furniture can stand the test of time in both durability and appeal.

2

the magic of color

Ask any kid whether he or she has a favorite color, and you're likely to get a resounding "yes!" Children are naturally drawn to color, and most will have a top choice before they are old enough to start school. What's more, they can be very unwavering in their preferences. You may have painted the nursery in shades of sage and yellow, but by the time your child is in kindergarten, she might be lobbying for pink and purple. Certainly by the time she's a preteen, expect your child to insist on a color palette that expresses her personality as a young adult.

Experts say that babies are better able to distinguish different shapes and contrasts rather than colors. Perhaps black and white is more interesting to a newborn, who may miss subtle contrasts until his eyes fully develop. But it won't be long before your child loves bright colors.

LEFT
This room is alive with bold color. If your child's tastes change, linens are easy and inexpensive to replace.

LEFT
With late-night feedings and changes, parents spend nearly as much time in the nursery as the newborn. That's why the room should be soothing for mom and dad as well as baby.

ABOVE
Every child perceives color differently. A bold wall like this one may not say "rest" to you, but it can tickle a little one pink.

If you've planned a soft pastel palette for your baby's room, don't worry: you can add bright colors and contrasts through toys, linens, and accessories later. In fact, some older babies may need the calming effect of soft colors rather than the stimulation of bold, primary hues. The bottom line: use the colors you like best in the nursery. For the most part, the only things that matter to your baby now are sleep and the next feeding.

If your child is a little older but not quite ready to choose a favorite color, there are clues you can observe. For example, look at her drawings. Is there a dominant color that you see repeatedly? What does she like to wear most? Most kids choose clothes based on color preference. Make a game of it. Sit down with your child, and ask her to pick out her favorite colored blocks and organize them by preference. You can do this with crayons, markers, paints, toys, or any other multicolored resource around the house. Sometimes a special object, such as a much-loved blanket or quilt, a poster or framed print, a cartoon character, or a favorite stuffed animal, can inspire an idea for a color accent or even an entire room's color scheme.

By the time most children are three or four years old, they have developed definite color preferences. Typically, they'll gravitate toward bright hues. (Not every little girl favors pink and purple.) Their tastes start to become more sophisticated, sometimes even offbeat, as they enter their adolescent and teen years.

Should you insist that the colors chosen by your kids for their rooms coordinate with the scheme you've selected for the rest of the house? That's entirely up to you. But even the most outlandish color preferences can be expressed, if not on every surface in the room, at least in linens, in accessories, or on walls that can easily be repainted later. Perhaps plain-white walls may seem unimaginative and boring. But neutral surfaces allow you to introduce an unlimited number of colors and patterns in other ways. Plus, there's the advantage of being able to change the entire look of a room by simply hanging new curtains or switching colors in a bedspread or quilt. All-white walls also let your trend-conscious youngster introduce a few faddish colors or posters to the room that can be discarded inexpensively when something new comes along.

One of the smartest things you can do before committing to a color scheme is to learn how to use color effectively, and with professional flair.

ABOVE
An offbeat palette is a fine choice for a kid's room and doesn't have to clash with the scheme you've chosen for the rest of the house. The trick is to keep the intensity of the color even.

BELOW
A whimsical piece of furniture can become a central motif when you echo its lines and hues elsewhere in the room.

smart tip

PICK YOUR PALETTE

Unpainted or "raw wood" furniture in pine or oak can be less costly than finished pieces and allows you to custom design the color scheme. Mixed pieces will appear to match when painted similarly. Because lots of kids love to paint, a well-planned painting project is a great way to include an older child or teen in the redesign of his room.

how color works

Light reflected through a prism creates a rainbow, known as the "color spectrum." Each band of color blends into the next, from red to ultraviolet. The longest band is red, then orange, yellow, green, blue, and violet. Color theory takes those bands and forms them into a circle known as a color wheel in order to show the relationship of one color to another.

The color wheel includes primary colors (red, blue, and yellow), secondary colors (green, orange, violet), and tertiary colors (red-orange, blue-green, for example). Secondary colors are made by mixing two primaries (blue and yellow make the secondary color green). A primary color and a secondary color mixed together make a tertiary color, (primary blue and secondary green make the tertiary color turquoise).

Colors vary in their intensity—that is, the level of the color's purity or saturation. The primaries, secondaries, and tertiaries represent colors at their full intensity. There are several ways to lessen a color's intensity. You can lighten it with white

color wheel combinations

The color wheel is a useful tool for pairing colors. Basically, it presents the spectrum of hues as a circle. The primary colors (yellow, blue, and red) are combined in the remaining colors (orange, green, and violet). The following are the most often used configurations for creating color schemes.

to form a tint, darken it with black to create a shade, or add gray to arrive at a tone. In addition to changing the intensity of a color, these methods affect what is known as the color's value. Value is the lightness or darkness of a color. Tinting gives a color a lighter value; shading gives it a darker value. A hue is simply another term for color or a family of colors.

Putting the Color Wheel to Work for You

Color schemes are developed by combining colors, using their relationship to one another on the color wheel as a guide. Once you've decided on a basic or main color, you can develop an outstanding scheme around it. Use the color wheel to help you envision certain color combinations for your child's room.

Monochromatic schemes are the easiest to develop because they use just one color; examples include totally pink rooms or totally blue rooms. You can use the color in various intensities and with different textures and patterns to create interest. To freshen the look of a monochromatic scheme over the years, all you have to do is change the accent colors. Introduce new colors with accessories or new curtains, for example.

Analogous schemes are invariably pleasing, as well as easy to develop, because they use colors that are next to one another on the color wheel. An example of an analogous color scheme is pink (technically, red tinted with white) and purple (actually, violet-red) a popular combination with young girls. Another combination, one that is often favored for boys, is blue and green-blue. You can play with variations in value, intensity, and texture to add interest to these color schemes.

Complementary schemes are achieved by using two colors that are directly opposite each other on the color wheel. Two such hues are also called contrasting colors. A bright-blue-and-orange bedroom? Well, yes, in full intensity the combination of these two contrasting colors might be hard to stomach, but consider a powdery blue room with pale peach-tone accents. The same complements in varying intensities can make an attractive, soothing combination, while equal amounts of both colors create conflicting tension. The dominance of one color, however, helps to settle things down.

Complementary schemes tend to be livelier than others. They consist of a pleasing balance of warm and cool. Strong contrasts may need some tempering, which you can apply by

color basics

Use color effectively to enhance the perception of the space itself. Make a large room feel cozy with warm colors, which tend to advance. Conversely, open up a small room with cool colors or neutrals, which tend to recede. The less-intense version of a color will generally reduce its tendency to advance or recede, as well. Other tricks: sharp contrasts often have the same impact as a dark color, reducing perceived space. Monochromatic schemes enlarge space. Neutrals of similar value make walls appear to retreat.

adding a lot of neutral surfaces or by starting with a neutral background (walls) and then using complementary accent colors in fabrics and accessories.

Triadic schemes consist of three or more colors equidistant on the color wheel. Imagine a nursery decorated in palest pink, blue, and yellow. True primaries of red, blue, and yellow often dominate preschoolers' rooms, where everything from toys to storage accessories are splashed in these colors.

Split-complementary schemes come together when you combine one color with the colors on both sides of the first color's complementary colors. An example is the combination of violet with orange-yellow and yellow-green.

Tetrad schemes are composed by combining any two pairs of complementary colors—for example, orange and blue with red and green.

So far, you've been thinking about color in terms of personal preference, but there are other things to keep in mind when making a choice. For example, warm hues (red, yellow, orange, peach, and cream) tend to energize the atmosphere. They're a good choice in places where there's a lot of activity. Cool hues (blue, violet, and green) are more restful. They work well in a room intended for relaxing and unwinding. Your child will play and sleep in his room, so try to find a pleasing balance of both. If he's active and finds it hard to settle down at nap time, predominantly warm hues may be too stimulating. A restful blue or a calming green may be better in this case.

Light and Color

Lighting can alter color dramatically. The quality of natural light changes through the course of the day, too. Consider this when you choose color for your child's room. Paint some test samples on the wall, and watch how the colors shift throughout the day. Do they need adjustment? Rooms with northern exposures will be filled with bluer, cooler light, which weakens warm colors but intensifies cool hues. Rooms with windows that face south will have a warmer, yellowish light. Rooms with windows that face east are sunny in the morning, while those with a western exposure bring in the late afternoon sun. Other factors, such as window treatments and artificial light sources, can alter these conditions. Although these generalizations are not absolute, they are a good place to start.

smart tip

LIGHT BRIGHT

For many folks, kids included, sun exposure is essential to a healthy, happy outlook. Those deprived of enough UV light can suffer from a condition called winter blues or Seasonal Affective Disorder (SAD). Luckily, there are light bulbs that imitate the kind of light the sun provides and can alleviate the symptoms of SAD, which include listlessness and even depression. Full-spectrum lights are available in floor and desk-lamp models, as well as light box units that stand on the floor or tabletop. Increasing outdoor activities and regular exercise are also ways to combat SAD.

ABOVE
Control light with a room-darkening shade. When sun is scarce, look for adjustable window treatments that allow you to maximize your natural light exposure.

OPPOSITE
Walls painted light yellow brighten a room that doesn't get too much natural light. Consider the exposure of the room before choosing colors.

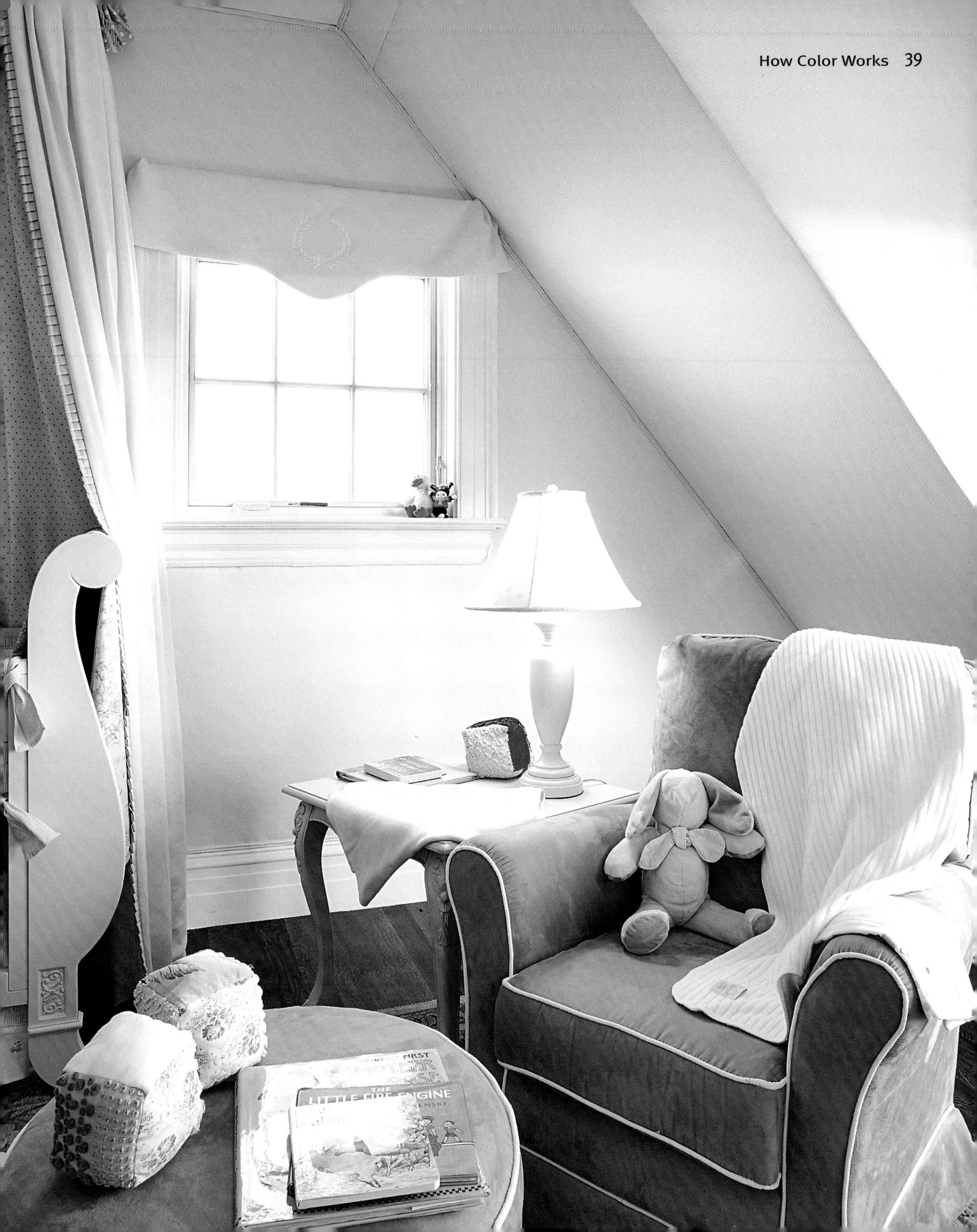
THE
LITTLE FIRE ENGINE

pattern

Pattern is another way to add personality to a room, establish a theme, visually alter the size or shape of the space, or camouflage minor surface imperfections. You can introduce pattern in a variety of ways—wallpaper and fabric being the two most popular. Because pattern is largely a vehicle for color, the same rules that guide the selection of color effectively narrow the field when it comes to choosing a pattern or a complement of patterns. Scale, as discussed on pages 16 and 19 in Chapter 1, is another important consideration.

Large-scale patterns are like warm colors in that they appear to come toward you. They can create a lively and stimulating atmosphere and generally make a large space seem cozier. In a small room, handle a large-scale pattern with care if you don't want to overpower the space—or your child. That doesn't mean rule it out completely, but perhaps use it sparingly. Small-scale patterns appear to recede, making small spaces seem larger. They can also be used to effectively camouflage odd angles or corners, such as eaves. Try a subtle, nondirectional pattern for this kind of application. In a large room, a small pattern can get lost, unless it contrasts sharply with the background color.

For interest, try to vary the scale of patterns. In general, use large-print fabrics on similar-scale furnishings, medium prints on medium-size pieces, and small prints on accent items. Rules, however, can always be broken. Case in point: you want to include a large upholstered chair in your teenage daughter's relatively small room. Choose a small print to de-emphasize the scale of the piece. Conversely, you found a small, old ottoman at a garage sale that would make a terrific accent piece in the room. Cover it in a large-scale print fabric to call attention to it.

When you think about it, applying the ideas of scale and proportion to pattern selection is really a matter of using your own common sense.

How to Mix Patterns

It's not as difficult to mix patterns as it looks, especially if you shop for coordinated lines of fabric and wallpaper, which take the guesswork—and the intimidation—out of using more than one pattern in a room. If you prefer to mix your own patterns, provide links with scale, color, and motif. The regularity of checks, stripes, textural looks, and geometrics (if they are small and low-contrast) tends to make them easy-to-mix "neutrals." A small checked pattern can play off a thin ticking stripe, while a strong plaid may require a bold stripe as a same-scale foil. The most effective link between disparate patterns is shared colors that are of a similar level of intensity—all pastel tones, for example. A solid-color fabric that pulls out a hue that is shared by more than one pattern in the room provides another way of establishing a visual connection.

smart tip

MIRROR, MIRROR

Look at a mirror not just as a bedroom necessity, but as a design opportunity. Use it to reflect a pattern, color, motif, texture, or even a light source you want to emphasize. If a room is particularly small, a well-placed mirror can open up the space. Some manufacturers even offer acrylic-based mirrors that won't shatter should playtime become too rambunctious.

LEFT
This wallpaper's small, interplanetary print can give a little astronaut the illusion of floating in outer space. A blue painting over the bed and similarly hued blinds anchor the main color of the room. Don't overlook toys as accent pieces, such as the wooden-rocket collection here.

TOP
This mirror certainly doesn't "match" the patterned wallpaper in color or design, but there's no denying how well the two work together. The match is made by a shared intensity of color and similar floral motif.

texture

Texture doesn't have the obvious impact on a room that color and pattern wield. Yet how a material feels, as well as how it looks, is important. The easiest way to incorporate texture into a design is with fabric. Obviously, you won't be using brocades and damasks in your child's room; you'll want something that's sturdy and washable but soft to the touch. Cottons and chenilles are good choices for curtains and bedding. Fabrics, however, are just the beginning. Tactile interest or texture can emanate from any material that is coarse or smooth, hard or soft, matte or shiny, but you should avoid anything that is very rough and can injure a child. Coarse and matte surfaces, such as some carpeting and cork, absorb light and sound. Glossy and smooth surfaces, which range from metal and glass to silk and enamel, reflect light.

Texture can alter a room spatially. Coarse or matte surfaces will make a room seem smaller and cozier. The glossy surfaces of some contemporary bedroom furniture can seem cold and uninviting without a cozy quilt on the bed to add warmth and contrast. Smooth and shiny surfaces do the reverse—they make space appear larger and brighter. A room that looks confined, for instance, may open up with the addition of a large mirror or a light-color floor. Light reflected off either one will brighten the room.

Keep in mind that texture also affects pattern and color. With fabrics, texture can either soften or intensify a pattern. With paint, a coarse texture subdues the intensity of the color, but adds subtle variations and shadings. On the other hand, a highly polished or glossy finish heightens a color.

You can improve relatively featureless rooms by adding contrasting textures with wallpaper or paint finishes, or through architectural embellishments such as cornices, crown moldings, and wainscoting. Window treatments are another natural place for texture. Fabric choices for draperies and curtains as well as the fabrics and other materials available for blinds and shades are enormous and varied. Texture can also be enhanced by the way fabric is hung. Pleating, for example, creates a play of light and shadow. You can combine layers of fabric, or fabric with blinds or shades, to add depth and and interest and show off different textures.

Carpets can be smooth or sculpted, while area rugs, wood, or cork are warming texture options.

OPPOSITE
The wicker baskets filled with soft goods break up the solid surfaces of this cubby. By backing the cubbies directly against the wall, the pretty wallpaper remains part of the picture.

LEFT
Babies and young children often comfort themselves by running their fingers along a favorite blanket or stuffed toy. But reserve beaded and embellished fabrics such as these for an older child's room.

smart steps
pulling it all together

Step 1 CREATE A SAMPLE BOARD
Use white foam-core presentation board, available in art-supply stores. A piece that measures 8½ x 11 inches is ideal. Glue swatches of fabric, paint-color chips, and wallpaper samples to it. Designate about two-thirds of it for the wall and window treatments, and divide the remaining third between the furnishings (including bed linens) and flooring. Add and remove things as you experiment with different looks, and view the sample board at different times of the day, under various light conditions.

Step 2 DEVELOP THE COLOR SCHEME
Bringing all you now know about color to bear, pick one main hue. Look at its complement or triad on the color wheel, and choose an accent or two. Go to the paint store, and get sample color chips of each of the colors in every intensity you can find so that you can play around until you find the combination that pleases you best.

Step 3 GET FABRIC AND WALLPAPER SAMPLES
You can often pull out a main color from these sources. Look at the way they're mixed in the sample books at the store. Professionals get a lot of their ideas by trial and error. Purchase a few samples, and do a little experimentation of your own.

Step 4 REVIEW THE BASIC PRINCIPLES OF SCALE, PROPORTION, LINE, BALANCE, HARMONY, AND RHYTHM
If you keep these in mind along with the physical makeup of the space, you can't go wrong. Play with different looks until you get it right.

design workbook
PLAYING WITH COLOR

primary importance

Primary colors need not be over-whelming. Here, deep-blue walls are a soothing backdrop to the painted playhouse and red accents.

store more

The carpeted play platform is a fun focal point, and it opens up the opportunity for plenty of storage with its roomy, built-in drawers.

on their level

The corner media cabinet, top left, puts the television exactly at kid level. Baskets and buckets hold toys and supplies.

mom's toys

A well-heeled playroom, left, includes furniture, phone, and an internet hookup for older kids.

soft serve

Kids spend lots of time on the floor, so comfort-able carpeting or rugs are essential. Bright, funky rock-ing chairs have no hard edges.

design workbook
LET THE COLOR WHEEL SPIN

red lite

In this girly bedroom, softened primaries create an even sweeter retreat. Yellow and blue shine through and the red bows out to its calmer cousin, pink. Plenty of white in the carpeting, fabrics, furniture, and trim keeps the pink from becoming overwhelming.

small comfort

A loveseat, top left, provides a cozy niche for story time. Select a style with a fold-out bed, which will come in handy when she's old enough for sleepovers.

catch a frill

Shelves with a scalloped edge, left, echo the toybox trim. Pegs put pretty purses on display instead of hiding them away in a closet. The bunny lamp on the dresser pairs nicely with the adorable chandelier over the bedside table.

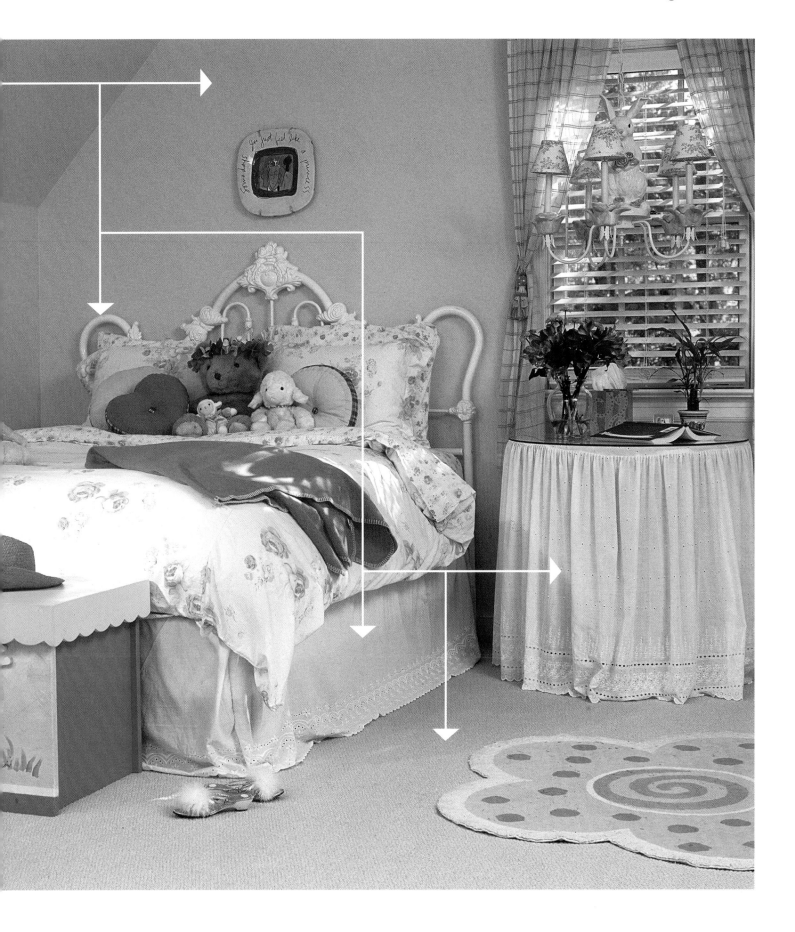

3

great furniture

When you're considering furniture, remember that there are scaled-down pieces designed just for young children. But for most families, a more practical choice is furniture that can grow with the child, such as a changing table that can be converted into a chest of drawers or standard-size furniture that will last through the teen years and into adulthood. You might also consider mixing different sizes and types of furniture. For example, you could combine a pint-size table and chairs or a small upholstered piece with a full bed. A small wardrobe with child-friendly shelves, hooks, and a hanging bar is another practical option.

LEFT
With a full-size bed below and a twin above, this bunk set maximizes sleeping capacity in this lively room.

Whether they're filled with books, toys or accessories, bookshelves come in handy in any kid's room. And don't forget a comfy chair or sofa where parents and kids can settle in to read or play a game.

sleeping arrangements

Newborns often feel more secure in a cozy bassinet until they are big enough to move into a regular crib, usually after a few months. (Refer to Chapter 5, "Decorating the Nursery," beginning on page 100, for advice about how to select and outfit a crib.) Around the age of two, most children are ready for the big step of sleeping in a bed, although this change may take place earlier or later. You'll know when the time is right by observing your child. Typically, the signal is when he is able to climb out of the crib on his own. In general, the Sleep Products Safety Council recommends making the transition from a crib to a bed by the time a child is 35 inches tall.

When you shop, select a bed and mattress wisely. These major purchases will affect both the comfort and safety of your child.

Beds and Mattresses

Along with proper nutrition and exercise, a good night's sleep is essential for your child's well-being. Kids do a lot of important things while they're asleep: growing, building new cells, energizing their organs and muscles, and processing all that they have learned today while improving their brain's capacity to learn more tomorrow. If kids don't sleep well, they'll be cranky, lethargic, and stressed out—pretty much the way you feel when you haven't had enough rest.

One way to make sure your child sleeps properly is to buy him a quality bed and mattress. While price isn't always an indication of quality, it's reasonable to assume that if something is cheap, the manufacturer cut corners somewhere along the line. And there's one area you should never skimp on: the quality of the mattress. The Better Sleep Council offers good advice for finding a quality, affordable mattress. (See the opposite page.)

In this chapter, you will find all of the general information you'll need to know in order to shop for and choose furniture wisely. You'll also find useful facts about lighting and light fixtures.

In addition to a comfortable crib or bed, your child will need lots of options for storing her books, toys, and other favorite things, as well as a place to keep her clothes. Because you can't expect a child to hang up her clothes if she can't reach the clothes rod, you'll want furniture that meets her needs as she grows. Chapters 5 through 8 will describe the specific furniture requirements for each age category.

Must you follow all of this advice to the letter? As with so many other decorating questions, the answer is always a personal one. Decide what you can afford to spend on furniture and accessories; then do what you feel is best for you and your child.

ABOVE
A quality bed and mattress is essential to a good night's sleep. Studies show that children who sleep well have improved moods and do better in school.

smart steps
nighty-night

Step 1 SHOP FOR SUPPORT

According to the Better Sleep Council, a good mattress and foundation should support the spine along its natural curve. Take your child with you when you shop. Have her lie down on the mattress with a pillow under her head; then slip your hand, palm-side down, under her back. A gap indicates that the mattress is too hard; likewise, having to force your hand under the child's back is a sign that the mattress is too soft.

Step 2 ASK ABOUT COIL COUNT

The number of innersprings (coils) determines support and durability in a mattress. The larger the bed (ranging from twin-size through king-size), the more coils. For a twin-size mattress, shop for one with at least 200 coils; adequate coil count for a double-size mattress is 300. Better mattresses have coil counts around 550; the coil count for a top-of-the-line mattress is 700.

Step 3 COMPARE UPHOLSTERY OPTIONS

Upholstery greatly influences the cost of a mattress and how cushiony or soft it feels. It doesn't affect the more important issue of support, however. Expensive mattresses typically feature fiber-filled cushions; more affordable are those with good-quality, high-density foam, cotton, or wool.

Step 4 INQUIRE ABOUT MATERIALS

According to the Better Sleep Council, only "29 states and the District of Columbia have laws requiring mattress manufacturers to identify mattresses constructed with new materials." That means that unless you see that assurance on the label, ask your retailer about it; make sure that the sleep set (mattress and foundation) you purchase is new and not refurbished.

Step 5 ASK THE SALESPERSON TO EXPLAIN THE WARRANTY

Don't expect a mattress to last more than about 12 years. (Some experts think 7 years.) A warranty protects you only against poor workmanship and defects.

ABOVE
It is especially important to choose a comfortable mattress in a bunk bed, which does not have the extra support of a box spring.

BELOW
Allow kids to try out mattresses and pick the one they find comfortable; no need to have the same mattress top and bottom.

Today, many parents are choosing double beds for their kids, even when the room isn't shared. This is a practical choice as children get older and want to entertain friends; the larger bed offers extra seating and lounging space for playing games, listening to music, or watching TV. Another option is a daybed with a trundle or pop-up mattress that rolls under the bed when not in use. This type of bed is popular with teenagers because it can also double as a sofa.

When two children share a room, it's better to have a separate bed for each one. If there isn't room for two twin-size beds, bunk beds offer a solution. Another space-saving idea is a loft bed, which typically features a twin-size bed that is elevated off the floor and rests on a platform. These beds are versatile: some models also come in double and queen sizes. You can pair a loft bed with a standard twin-size bed that can slip under the loft to create an L-shape arrangement in a room. Other types may have built-in storage, a desk, or a playhouse underneath.

Beds come in numerous furniture styles and finishes. Check the frame and construction, and look for safety labels. Run your hand around the frame and headboard to feel for sharp edges, harmful protrusions, or chips or nicks in the finish. Make sure there are no gaps between the mattress, headboard, and frame that are wide enough for little fingers to get caught. Shake the frame and any rails to test for sturdiness, and make sure your child's head can't get stuck between spindles in the headboard. If you're shopping for a very young child's bed, you may want to inquire about optional side rails, which are detachable.

With bunk beds or a loft bed, nothing should wobble; periodically examine all of the bolts and screws, and tighten them immediately if they're loose. Check that the ladder is securely attached to the top bed and that it's at a comfortable angle for climbing. Always install a guardrail on any side that isn't against a wall. Note the headroom. A child on the top bunk should be able to sit up comfortably without hurting himself; likewise a child in the bottom bed should be able to sit up without hitting his head on the bed above him.

Good-quality beds are constructed with sturdy metal or wood frames. Models made of particleboard are less expensive, but you get what you pay for. In the case of some whimsical styles, such as the "sports car" bed, it makes sense to pay less because your child will outgrow the novelty of it in a few years anyway. However, a well-built one can be passed along to a younger sibling.

LEFT
Building this bed into the wall creates a cozy sleeping niche while also saving floor space.

RIGHT
These bunks are another clever use of space under the eaves. Make sure bunk-bed mattresses are not too thick for the guardrails.

Headboards and Footboards. These decorative accents may be optional, but they help to establish style. In most cases, the bed is the room's focal point—the most dominant feature because it's often the largest object there. A handsome headboard, with or without a matching footboard, can make a dramatic or whimsical design statement that sets the tone for the entire room.

You can purchase a matching headboard (and footboard) when you buy a suite of coordinated bedroom furniture, but it's more interesting to choose something that's not "matchy-matchy." Handsome pairings might include a painted metal bed with laminate storage pieces; iron with mellow maple or oak; or wicker combined with painted wood. By mixing finishes and materials this way, you're adding textural variety and personalizing the decor.

Basic bedstead styles include solid, carved, or curved panels, spindles, slats, spokes, or posts. Spindles and spokes can be short or tall (called a "tester bed"), perfect for a canopy. Beds can be customized with fabric or upholstery. And, unlike mattresses, you can refinish an old headboard with a decorative finish, such as a stenciled design or a decoupaged motif. But sometimes, all you'll need is a fresh coat of paint.

TOP LEFT
A day bed with an elegant side table sets a ladylike tone for this room.

TOP RIGHT
This carved-wood headboard in deep blue complements the nautical theme here.

LEFT
A headboard with built-in storage looks good and serves a useful function.

OPPOSITE
A regal four-poster bed paired with a mosquito-netting coronet would tickle any princess pink.

mattresses

When you're recycling an old bed, always buy a new mattress and foundation (typically a box spring), for the sake of cleanliness and your child's orthopedic health. An old mattress is already molded to the previous user's shape, and although it may look clean, it probably harbors dust mites and bacteria.

It's also not a good idea to use a new mattress over an old foundation. You may actually shorten the life span of the mattress this way. Mattress and foundation sets are designed to work together for comfort's sake, so don't try to save a few dollars by buying one and not the other.

If you're considering an antique bed, be prepared to pay for a custom-made mattress and foundation. Today's standard-size mattresses and foundations probably won't fit your vintage bed. Check the measurements of the bed ahead of time. And remember, there are lots of reproductions in stores that work with today's mattress sizes.

case goods

Storage furniture, referred to as case goods in the furniture industry, is available as built-in, modular, or freestanding units. Before you make up your mind about any of these options, it's a good idea to shop around, compare prices, check quality, and think hard about your son or daughter's storage needs, always erring on the side of too much rather than too little.

You might also consider how long you plan to use the furniture. Will this be an investment that has to last from early childhood through the teen years and, perhaps, into college? How much abuse do you think it will have to take, and how much time are you willing to invest in its maintainence? If you know the furniture is going to take a beating, but still has to last, invest in something that's well-constructed and has a tough finish.

Built-In Furniture

Built-in furniture is an especially good solution for an oddly shaped room because you can have it custom-designed for the space. This kind of made-to-measure storage also allows you to tailor the cabinet interiors to suit your child's particular needs. For example, if he requires racks to hold sporting equipment, your carpenter or contractor can outfit a special cabinet for this purpose. However, custom-made furniture can be expensive. It's a good idea to seek several estimates before hiring someone to build it for you. Get references, preferably from people you know who have worked with the person, and ask to see examples of his or her work.

One way you might be able to save some money is if you purchase stock cabinetry that can be retrofitted into the space, just like kitchen cabinetry. In fact, you should price stock kitchen cabinets, especially discontinued lines that are often discounted. But speak to your contractor or carpenter about this before buying anything to make sure this plan is feasible.

Modular Systems

Like modular seating, modular storage systems consist of separate, coordinated units that can be purchased individually or as an entire suite. Modular systems have the look of built-in furniture but, unless custom-made, they're usually more affordable. Of course, price is determined by the number of pieces, the finish you choose, and whether assembly is required.

Modular furniture can be used to create storage walls or room dividers, and it can be very convenient when you have to divide one room between two children. Storage walls are connected units that fit from floor to ceiling. They divide space while providing access to storage from one or both sides. Room dividers serve a similar purpose, but do not extend to the ceiling or even from wall to wall.

It's best to purchase this type of furniture after you've seen it yourself in a showroom. Check for sturdiness, and make sure that hinges and supports are strong. Run your hands across the finish to make sure that it's smooth. If the furniture is for a nursery or a young child's room, inspect it for sharp corners and edges, choosing pieces with rounded corners whenever possible. Examine the shelving. It should be strong enough to hold a large number of books, and adjustable so that you can install it at a safe and comfortable height for your child. Avoid anything with glass doors. Even if it's shatterproof, glass picks up fingerprints and smudges, which means more work for you. Glass is great, but not for kids.

If you have to assemble the furniture yourself, find out if you need better-than-average skills and what tools are required. If the furniture comes in pieces ready to be carried away, can you fit the boxes into your car? Sometimes you can pay the store for assembly, but that could mean you must have the furniture delivered—for an additional fee.

smart tip CASE GOODS

The furniture industry uses a variety of labels to denote the materials used in a case-goods furniture item.
The meanings of these terms are regulated by the Federal Trade Commission.
- Solid wood (i.e., "solid oak" or "solid pine") means that the exposed surfaces are made of wood without any veneer or plywood. Other woods may be used on unexposed surfaces, such as drawer sides and backs.
- Genuine wood means that all exposed parts of the furniture are made of a veneer of the wood over hardwood or plywood.
- Wood means that none of the parts of the furniture are made of plastic, metal, or other materials.
- Man-made materials refers to plastic-laminate panels that are printed to look like wood. The furniture may also include plastic molded to look like wood carving or trim.

ABOVE
Where closets are small, custom cabinetry can provide extra storage that is attractive and exactly where you need it.

OPPOSITE
With open shelving above and cabinetry below, this wall yields ample storage and valuable counter space as well.

Freestanding Furniture

Generally, dressers and chests are categorized by their storage capacity. The smallest is a lingerie chest, followed by the drawer chest. The door chest is larger still, with drawers at the bottom and two doors at the top. The armoire, or wardrobe, is the largest "chest" available. A clothes rod inside defines it as a wardrobe.

You might also want to include a nightstand on either side of your child's bed. This can be a small table or chest with a drawer and a cabinet. The nightstand is perfect for holding a reading lamp, a phone, a clock, and maybe even a framed picture of Mom and Dad.

Depending on the size of the room, other options include open shelving, cabinets with hinged or sliding doors, and drawers in many shapes and sizes. Almost every child has a collection—whether it's dolls, seashells, sports memorabilia, or funny hats. Some storage pieces offer a display area for collections or a place to protect valuable items from the sun.

ABOVE
These scallop-edge pieces happen to match, but freestanding furnishings don't have to come from a set to look great.

LEFT
Including an ample desktop and sturdy chair in the design emphasizes the idea that schoolwork is serious business.

OPPOSITE
A uniquely styled chest of drawers like this might tempt you to demand that they "file" their clothes.

good furniture construction

Furniture can be constructed of hardwood or softwood. Hardwoods are often used in high-quality furniture because they are stronger than softwoods. Hardwoods come from deciduous trees, such as cherry, maple, oak, ash, pecan, teak, walnut, mahogany, and poplar. Softwoods are from conifer trees, such as fir, pine, redwood, cedar, and cypress. The wood has to be well-seasoned and kiln-dried before it is put to use, or it will split and splinter easily.

Veneers are thin sheets of hardwood that are glued to a core of less expensive material. Once associated with inferior quality, veneers are more acceptable today and may be stronger than solid wood. Wide boards of solid wood will warp and crack with weather changes; veneer over plywood will not.

The "solid wood" label allows use of composition boards, such as plywood and particleboard, in nonexposed areas of the furniture. You will find these materials used this way in moderately priced furniture. In the budget range, these materials may be used more extensively.

Joining Methods

Wood can be joined together with staples, nails, screws, joints, and glue. Several of these methods may be used in one piece of furniture. To evaluate quality, look for strong construction at the joints. Joints are where one part of a piece of furniture fits into another. They're usually glued together with synthetic glues or fastened with screws. Staples are used only on the most inexpensive furniture and should not be used to join any piece that bears weight. Nails are stronger than staples but not as strong as the following joining methods. If you intend to invest in a quality furniture piece, look for these types of construction.

Butt joints connect the edge of one piece of wood to the face of another. They are weak joints and should be used only in places that are not subject to stress, such as where a bureau top meets the frame. Using dowels makes stronger butt joints.

Miter joints are used at the corners of tables. The ends of the two pieces are angled to fit together to form a right angle. This joint should be reinforced with dowels, nails, or screws.

Tongue-and-groove joints are used to join two or more boards together side by side, as in a tabletop. A groove is cut into one side of a board, and a tongue carved out on the other. When placed side by side, the tongue of one board fits into the groove of the next, and so on.

Dovetail joints are used to join drawer sides. Notches cut into the ends of each piece should fit together smoothly.

Double-dowel joints use two dowels to peg joints together in case goods and to attach legs to the side rails of chairs.

Mortise-and-tenon joinery is the strongest method of joining pieces of wood at right angles. The end of one piece of wood is shaped to fit into a hole in the other, which distributes the weight and stress over a wide area.

Corner blocks may be set into joints and screwed in place to provide extra support.

OPPOSITE
Both kids can feel as it they have their own private space with this sturdy loft bed/lower bunk ensemble.

BELOW LEFT
A bentwood rocker with leather seating takes up little space but delivers big contemporary style in this nursery.

BELOW RIGHT
This storage unit rolls out of the way when extra floor space is needed to spread out toys, a puzzle, or a board game.

Finishes

Finishes such as stains, paints, and lacquers add color and protect the surface of a furniture piece. A clear finish allows the natural grain of the wood to show through, while stains will change the color of the wood. Depending upon which you choose, a finish can make your furniture look smooth or rustic.

Distressing is a popular method of making new wood look old. The wood is beaten and battered before the finish is applied, "aging" it and enhancing its rustic charm. This finish tends to hide any scratches or fingerprints on the furniture, which makes it a good choice for kids' rooms, where surfaces are liable to take a beating.

Painted finishes, also popular today, can be playful or artistic. Unlike a distressed finish, however, paint tends to highlight flaws in the wood. This makes painted pieces more expensive than ones with natural finishes because extra care must be taken at the factory to remove imperfections from the wood. If you plan to refinish an old piece of wood furniture, you can do the work yourself to save money. Depending on the shape it's in, restoring wood furniture requires various levels of skill. Sometimes, however, all it takes is re-gluing loose joints, filling in small nicks with wood filler, a light sanding, and a new stain or painted finish.

Finishes are definitely a matter of personal taste, but should always be strong enough to resist moisture. You can simply coat inexpensive pieces with a layer of polyurethane. The finishing of high-quality furniture includes sanding, glazing, waxing, and hand buffing. Become familiar with different finishes by comparing the look and feel of both inexpensive and expensive pieces. Make sure the surface is hard and smooth, with no bubbles, cracks, or uneven discoloration.

LEFT
This custom wood furniture is constructed of light ash and sealed with a clear, non-yellowing polyurethane finish.

BELOW
Parts of this desk and hutch combination were finished with a clear varnish. The rest was painted and antiqued.

OPPOSITE
Never underestimate the high impact of a furniture piece that's been painted in a bright color.

upholstered furniture

It's wonderful to include a comfortable upholstered piece in your child's bedroom if you have the space. Whether you're thinking of a window seat, an armchair and ottoman, a petite slipper chair, or even a small sofa or love seat, you should know some facts about upholstery before you shop.

When you buy upholstered furniture, you can often choose from a range of price levels, or grades, of fabric or coverings. These grades are assigned a letter from A to D on up, with A at the high-price end. Grading is determined by the quality of the materials, the amount of fabric needed to match the pattern at the seams, corners, and edges, and the source of the pattern design (a famous designer's pattern costs more). Luckily, upholstered furniture in this room won't be subjected to much of the hard use it would get in the family room, for example, so you may not have as much concern for structural and support elements (the frame, legs, and arms).

Because upholstery coverings affect the price of furniture more than any other element of construction, you may want to find ways to keep the price down. Consider the frame design, for example. Curves, such as those around arms or across the back, are more expensive to cover than straight lines. Large, complex patterns and prints are harder to match than small, overall fabric designs.

Details that include pleats and scalloped edging, and trimmings such as welts, braids, buttons, and fringe will add to the final cost as well.

Always inquire about an upholstery fabric's durability. In general, tightly woven fabrics wear best. Fabrics with woven-in patterns wear better than printed fabrics. Various natural and synthetic fibers offer numerous looks and textures and perform differently in terms of wear and tear. In a child's room, it makes sense to use a fabric that has been pretreated for stain resistance at the mill, but this will add to the price. Any coating that is sprayed on from a can will come off when you wash or even spot-clean, but you will save money by treating the fabric yourself with a spray-on product that you reapply as necessary.

Natural fibers. Cotton, linen, wool, and silk are made from natural materials. Cotton is soft and durable. However, its fibers will disintegrate under consistent exposure to direct sunlight. Keep that in mind if you're covering a window seat that's exposed to strong, direct sunlight. Cotton is also less stain resistant than synthetic fibers. Linen has a tailored, crisp feel and is one of the most durable fibers available. It is most often found in natural colors because it does not dye well. It, too, disintegrates in sunlight. Wool is extremely durable as well as abrasion- and stain-resistant, but should be mothproofed before use. Silk is a

beautiful, but fragile fabric. Soft and luxurious, it is difficult to clean and discolors under strong light. It's pretty obvious that silk is impractical for a child's room.

Synthetic fibers. Synthetic materials are alternatives to natural fibers, although they are often blended with them. Polyester is strong and easy to clean. It withstands direct sunlight and is flame- and abrasion-resistant. Rough in texture, it is often blended with natural fibers to soften its touch. It is a smart choice for a kid's room. Olefin is used to create heavy textured fabrics. It is a coarse and bulky fiber that is strong and stain resistant. However, it does not wear well under direct sunlight. Nylon is the strongest and most soil-resistant fiber. Recent developments in nylon give it the look and feel of wool. It, too, is sensitive to sunlight.

When shopping, read labels, compare the feel of different materials, and make sure your choices are flame resistant.

furniture quality

When shopping for case goods, you'll find varying levels of quality and pricing. Use this checklist to judge what you're getting for your money.

- New furniture should be tagged with the type of construction (solid or veneer) and woods used.
- Veneers and laminates should be well joined to the base material.
- Cabinet doors should work smoothly.
- Hinges and other hardware should be strong and secure.
- Drawers should fit well, open smoothly without binding, and have stops.
- Bottoms of drawers should be held by grooves, not staples or nails.
- Insides of drawers should be smooth and sealed.
- Corners of drawers should have dovetail joints.
- Weight-bearing joints should be reinforced with corner blocks.
- Back panels should be screwed into the frame.
- The finish should feel smooth (unless it is distressed).
- Long shelves should have center supports.

OPPOSITE
Washable cotton slipcovers unite all the colors of the room and make a mismatched chair and ottoman look made for each other.

ABOVE
An upholstered chair makes a great accent piece in a child's room. Make sure to choose a fabric that's been treated for stain resistance.

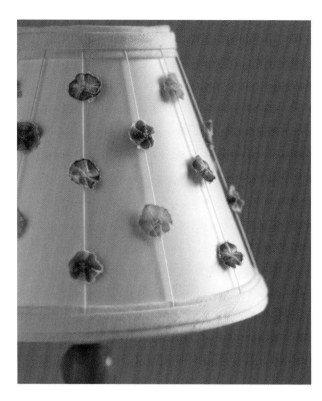

lamps and other lighting fixtures

Don't forget to include useful and efficient lighting fixtures in your design plan. For the best result, become familiar with the basic concepts behind good lighting design. There are three types of lighting to consider for any room: ambient, task, and accent lighting.

Ambient. The general illumination that fills the entire room is called ambient lighting. For the safety and comfort of your child's room, include sufficient amounts.

Task. Lighting that brightens a specific area, such as a desktop, is called task lighting. It is paramount, especially as children begin to read and do projects in their rooms.

Accent. Purely decorative illumination is called accent lighting. You can use it to spotlight a framed print on the wall or to highlight a collection that's displayed on a shelf.

In a nursery, you'll want lighting that works for you and your little one. You'll spend a lot of time there, helping him or her to dress, reading stories, and cuddling. Use a dimmer switch to brighten light when attending to the baby; then adjust it to a lower level for nighttime needs.

Over time, playing, doing homework, grooming, and other activities will require lighting that supports these more demanding visual tasks while avoiding eyestrain.

Ambient and Task Lighting

Wall sconces, recessed fixtures, and track lighting are excellent sources of ambient light. They're probably also the safest kinds of fixtures to use in a young child's room. With them, you don't have to worry about lamps tipping over when kids get

OPPOSITE
A table or dresser lamp with a whimsical, decorative shade is a popular choice for kids' rooms, but it needs to be balanced with other fixtures for task and general lighting.

LEFT
Besides a reading lamp, this nursery includes recessed-canister "star" fixtures in the ceiling that provide excellent ambient light.

ABOVE
Accent lights draped across the headboard posts are purely for pizzazz, while the flexible-arm desk lamp provides good illumination for homework.

rambunctious. Keeping any source of light out of reach of little hands can prevent burns.

Recessed fixtures combined with an adjustable-arm or gooseneck desk lamp are perfect in the work area because you can control glare and balance the general light with them. Never aim any light source directly onto the desk or work surface; angle it to avoid eye-straining glare.

Any lamp that's used in a child's room has to be designed so that it doesn't tip easily or produce high levels of heat that can be dangerous. Look for lamps that are not top heavy, are generally well-balanced, or can clip securely onto a desk. (Avoid floor lamps, which can be easily knocked over.) Opt for bright general lighting for kids who play on the floor during the early years. Add localized task lighting where children read, draw, or do crafts.

When kids are old enough to read in bed, an adjustable light near the bedpost is a good idea. Besides, a lamp near the bed makes it safer for kids who sometimes have to get up during the night. Night lights along the way to the bathroom are always helpful as well, especially to prevent tripping over toys and other items left on the floor. At the computer, provide both task and general lighting that is compatible with the screen at the child's height. The idea is to illuminate what is displayed on the monitor with task lighting, while using ambient light to eliminate the distracting contrast of what's on the screen and what is in the area behind it.

Reading in Bed

You can encourage your kids to read more if you make it comfortable to do so. Because they are smaller, children are naturally lower to the mattress than adults. Adjustable lamp arms should be positioned to best meet a child's needs. As kids get bigger, other types of fixtures are fine, but they must meet certain criteria.

Table lamps. Table lamps next to the bed should be no more than 32 inches high for comfort. The lamp should have a shade with a bottom circumference of 15 to 17 inches, a top circumference of 8 to 15 inches, and a depth from top to bottom of 6 to 14 inches. For reading, the lamp should line up with your child's shoulder (when propped up in a reading position), 22 inches to the side of the book's center, with the bottom of the shade 20 to 24 inches from the top of the mattress.

Wall-mounted or pendant lamps. Make the most of a tight space. Position them as you would a bedside lamp.

Dresser and Vanity Lamps

When you're selecting lamps for a child's dresser or vanity, you'll want ones that are both stylish and practical. If the lamps are for a large dresser with a mirror that will be used for grooming by an older child, select fixtures that measure 25 inches from the dresser top to the center of the shade. Generally, the shade's bottom circumference should be 11 to 14 inches, with a top circumference of 7 to 8 inches, and a depth of at least 7 to 9 inches from the top of the shade to the bottom.

Scale down for grooming at a vanity or dressing table. Select lamps that are 15 inches from the tabletop to the center of the shade. The best shade dimensions for this situation are a bottom that's 9 to 11 inches, a top minimum of 7 to 8 inches, and a depth of 9 inches. To keep it out of

sight and reduce glare, the bulb should be at least 2 inches below the top of the shade.

Although a reading lamp can use a 60- to 75-watt bulb, double dressers require lamps that are in scale with their size and produce more light. They may take up to 100 or 150 watts to make grooming easier.

By carefully considering all of the room's lighting requirements, you'll choose a fixture that combines both style and practicality.

OPPOSITE
Where there is no bedside table, a wall-mounted lamp makes sense. Observe your child reading in bed to determine how to adjust the lamp to avoid glare.

BELOW
Wall-mounted fixtures with articulated arms accommodate a variety of reading positions.

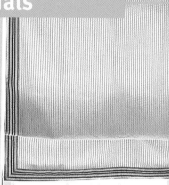

design workbook
SIGNS OF GOOD DESIGN

raw materials

Designed around a traffic-sign collection, the combination of wood and metal furnishings gives this room a funky, edgy feeling.

warm front

The rich red, yellow, blue, and green in the bedding and wall colors keep this room feeling cozy despite the abundance of metal furnishings and accessories.

pull up a pillow

A stack of generous cushions, top left, invites a group of friends to lounge on the floor and play.

know your lines

The simple lines of the classic metal chair, left, provides stylish support while working at the desk. The metallic finish looks snazzy.

design workbook
FUSION WITH COLOR AND STYLE

source of style

The delicate palette and the striped pattern used on the walls were inspired by the fabrics and trim on the carefully selected slip covers. (See also below left.)

strange bedfellows

Not a single piece of furniture in this nursery was originally part of a matched suite. But painted finishes and complementary fabrics blend everything together beautifully.

mix it up

The dresser and chest of drawers, above left, are different but complementary, thanks to the same pink shade of paint. Now, there's no doubt that they belong together.

4
walls, windows, and floors

WALL TREATMENTS   WINDOW TREATMENTS   FLOORING
DESIGN WORKBOOK

One of the easiest ways to transform any space into a personality-packed room is with new wall, window, and floor treatments. Wallpaper, paint, fabric, and area rugs are the perfect mediums for adding color, pattern, and texture to your child's room, and they are all reasonably affordable home improvements that you can do yourself. But while painting trimwork or putting up wallpaper are relatively easy projects that can be accomplished over a weekend, installing new hardwood floors or wall-to-wall carpeting is best left to a professional. Instead of cheap fabrics or the latest cartoon characters, stick with classic motifs and well-constructed materials. Consider maintenance and durability of wallpaper, fabric, and flooring options before buying. In this chapter, you'll learn about all of the decorative options available for your child's room.

LEFT
Sunlight pours into this already bright room, made extra cheerful and comfy thanks to its bold colors and retro shag carpeting.

wall treatments

You have two basic choices when it comes to walls: decorate them to make a dramatic statement, or let them act as an unobtrusive backdrop for the furnishings. If the furniture isn't particularly interesting, add pizzazz to the room with bold colors or patterns. On the other hand, a subtle palette won't take away from a beautiful bed or handsome, built-in furniture.

If the room lacks architectural interest, you can create eye-catching effects with either paint, wallpaper, or a combination of the two. Add a frieze (a band installed on the upper portion of the wall near the ceiling line) or a chair rail using a wallpaper border, for example. Or create a wainscot effect by painting the wall; then install wallpaper on the bottom half of the wall and a border at chair-rail height. Your only limitation is your imagination and the time and money you have to spend.

Paint

Paint is your easiest and least-expensive option. There is nothing like a fresh coat of paint to make a room look clean and new. The important thing to remember when buying paint is that there are different grades. In gen-

paint basics

Most interior paints are either alkyd-resin (oil-based) products or latex (water-based) varieties. Oil and water don't mix, and generally neither do the paints based on them. For multilayered effects, stick to one type or the other.

- Alkyd paints are somewhat lustrous, translucent, and hard-wearing. But alkyds, and the solvents needed for cleaning up, are toxic and combustible, requiring good work-site ventilation. Alkyds are better suited to special techniques such as combing and ragging, where glaze is brushed on in sections and then manipulated to create texture and special effects.
- Latex paints, which now approach alkyd's durability and textural range, are nontoxic, quick-drying, and clean up easily with soap and water. Most nonprofessionals find latex paint easier to work with and useful for creating many popular decorative finishes. In general, latex paints are best suited to effects that are dabbed on over the base coat, as in sponging or stenciling. Their short drying time can be an advantage because mistakes can simply be painted over and redone. Latex paint is usually the best choice for covering an entire wall because the job can be completed from start to finish in a few hours.

eral, the higher the grade, the better the quality—and the higher the price. Bargain paints aren't always a good deal: they don't offer the coverage that a better-grade product does, and you'll have to make up for that deficiency with additional coats—which mean extra gallons—of paint.

A custom color, achieved by taking a swatch of fabric to the paint store and asking for a perfect match, will be more expensive, but can often be worth the extra cost. (Never guess when it comes to color; even a slight variation can throw everything off balance.) Sheen will raise the price as well; in most cases, a glossy paint is more expensive than one with a flat finish. Designer and specialty paints, those that produce decorative effects or textures, are premium products that sometimes require special application tools as well. You might want to limit them to trim.

Flat paints are typically best for walls and ceilings, but they tend to mar easily, so you may not want to use them in a young child's room where the walls will get lots of fingerprints and other abuse. A semigloss finish, which has a higher sheen than a flat finish, will be easier to keep clean because you can wipe off most marks with a damp cloth and mild detergent.

Some paints are formulated and marketed specifically for kids' rooms, and they let you create fun effects with no particular professional skills. These products include glow-in-the-dark and glittery top coats, as well as blackboard paint that kids can write and draw on, and then erase. Just keep in mind that you may have to give the walls a light sanding before painting over some of these effects when you want to make a change later.

Wallpaper

Wallpaper can add instant style to your child's room and give you a headstart in developing the overall decorating scheme. Popular patterns include character themes, animals, sports motifs, and other collections that have been designed to appeal to young children. If your child is beyond this stage, you can select from a wide range of ready-made patterns that are suitable for any room in the house. In both cases, patterns are often designed to coordinate with other prints and fabrics. You can easily mix and match them to create a cohesive look not only for the walls, but for window treatments and bed dressings as well. But don't go overboard with mix-and-match prints. You want your child's room to reflect his unique personality, rather than look formulaic.

There are several types of wallcoverings on today's market. But when kids are involved, it's always practical to choose something that's marked *washable* and *scrubbable*. Generally, hand-painted, flocked, or embossed wallcoverings or woven grass-cloths are inappropriate for a child's room.

Vinyl coverings. Vinyl wallcoverings are hugely popular for kids' rooms because they can take a beating. Finger marks, grease, and moisture pose no threat to their long-lasting good looks. There are three types of vinyl wall products.

■ Paper-backed vinyl is plenty sturdy for kids' rooms, and is generally washable and peelable, which means that when your daughter gets too old for dancing teddy bears, you can remove the paper without difficulty. It's frequently sold prepasted, which makes it easier to apply, as well. Fortunately, most wallpaper patterns geared for kids' rooms are printed on paper-backed vinyl.

■ Fabric-backed vinyl has a vinyl top layer over fiberglass or cloth. It's tough, which means you can scrub crayon markings. This type is heavier than paper-backed vinyl, and it doesn't come prepasted.

■ Vinyl-coated paper is inexpensive, but it isn't as durable as the other vinyl options. Sticky, oily little hands will permanently mar it.

LEFT
This large-scale floral print might be too much for an entire bedroom, but it is just right for this small bath.

OPPOSITE
If you can imagine an effect, there is a wallpaper pattern available to achieve it. This one transforms the bedroom into a cozy log cabin.

When you're ready to select a pattern, don't forget the principles of scale and proportion, line, balance, rhythm, and harmony, which were discussed in Chapter 1. (See "Design Basics," page 19.) You might also review Chapter 2, "The Magic of Color," beginning on page 32, for additional advice. Naturalistic (floral) and stylized (repeated motif) patterns complement traditional schemes, whether they are formal or informal in style. Abstract and geometric patterns work well in contemporary settings. These rules are not hard and fast, however. A geometric pattern, such as a plaid, can be at home in a traditional or country room, and stripes look great with just about any decorating style. As a general guideline, a pattern that's too large for the room will usually overpower it. A large print may be acceptable or even dramatic in a powder room or a small foyer, because no one spends a lot of time in either place. However, a bold pattern would likely be too much for a small bedroom unless you limit its use to an accent wall, for example. Conversely, when a pattern is too small, it will seem to fade away.

smart tip

ESTIMATING PAINT AND WALLPAPER NEEDS

How much paint you need depends on the size of the room, the condition of the wall surface, and the paint's spreading rate, which is given on the manufacturer's label.

For a rough estimate of how much paint you'll need to cover the walls:

- Measure the total footage around the perimeter and multiply by the wall height in feet.
- From this subtract 20 square feet for each door and 14 square feet for each window.
- Divide by the spreading rate (usually 300 to 400 feet per gallon).

That's the number of gallons you'll need. Do a similar calculation for the ceiling by measuring the square footage and dividing by the spread rate.

To estimate how much paint is needed for the trim in a room, the rule of thumb is about one-fourth of what is required for the walls. It will be more or less, depending on the number of windows and doors and the amount of detail trim. If you need to get another gallon of paint mixed later, the color may be slightly different than that of the first batch.

To estimate how much wallpaper you'll need, determine the room's adjusted square footage, and then divide that number by 30. This takes into account the likely wastage from the standard 36 square feet in a roll. Round up to the nearest whole number for ordering standard rolls.

To be on the safe side, it's a good idea to borrow the wallpaper sample book. Some stores will allow you to take books home for a day or two, but they usually charge a small fee that is often refunded upon return. Otherwise, ask for a small cutting to take home. Better yet, buy one roll. Tape or tack it to the wall. Look at the sample at different times of the day, with light fixtures turned on and off, and with window treatments in place. This is the only way you can be sure that what you've selected will look the way you envisioned.

Following are a few ideas for using wallpaper.

■ Set off special areas with different patterns. Many prints come in reverse versions (a dark color on a light background versus a light color on a dark background). Try them to enhance architectural features such as alcoves or eaves.

■ Pick a theme that will coordinate easily with the room's other elements, such as bedding and curtains.

■ Use a peelable border over a plain wallpaper. As your child's tastes change, you can simply replace the border.

window treatments

You can accomplish a few objectives with window treatments. First, and most important, you can use them to strengthen or soften the window opening. You can highlight an attractive window, as well as a lovely view, or play down elements that are less than pleasing. Window treatments also provide an opportunity for introducing more color and pattern into the room, while allowing you to control natural light and provide privacy and insulation. Even if a room has small windows, it can be cheerful and relatively bright if you select the right window treatment. Conversely, a room with large, drafty windows can be made more comfortable when the windows are dressed to keep the cold out but let in the sunshine.

There are many types of window treatments from which to choose, including a range of curtains, shades, blinds, and shutters. By combining or layering different treatments, you can achieve the greatest versatility. Pair sheers with lined, adjustable panels, or a simple valance with blinds or shutters. You can purchase most window fashions in ready-made, standard sizes. Or if your budget allows, you can custom-order them to the windows' specifications or to match treatments with a bedding or wallpaper pattern. You'll find a variety of options in today's market.

LEFT
A simple blind or shade for privacy topped with a valance that complements the decor is often all that's needed in a child's room.

ABOVE
An ordinary window can become a focal point with a cornice or pelmet that is constructed of wood or cardboard and attached to the window frame.

OPPOSITE
A beautiful window can shine on its own with just a light dressing for privacy.

Curtains and Valances. Curtains made from washable fabrics (typically a cotton and polyester blend) need minimal care. But if your child has allergies or a sensitivity to fabric sizing or synthetics, it's wiser to select a fabric that's 100 percent natural. Remember that cotton curtains need to be lined in order to be fade-resistant, an important consideration if the windows receive strong exposure to the sun.

Depending on the decorating style of the room and the size and shape of the windows, you may choose between short or long, ruffled or plain panels; café styles; sheer or solid fabrics; tab-top, pleated, or gathered headings; and swagged, pouffed, ballooned, or festooned valances. While traditional and country decors can carry off fussier treatments, contemporary-style rooms require the simplicity of a tailored or pared-down styles.

Curtains are always a great choice because you can easily coordinate them with the color or print used on the walls and bed linens; they also lend a soft, cozy feeling to the room. If lined, curtains can block out drafts and harsh sunlight. Among their disadvantages is that they collect dust and may require professional cleaning. They also must be completely closed to adequately keep out strong sunlight and prevent unpleasant drafts.

Blinds. Whether they're made of metal, wood, or vinyl, blinds effectively block the sun when they're closed. Today's styles include a wide selection of colors, textured-fabric finishes, and the choice of vertical or horizontal slats in standard, mini, or micro widths. You can pair blinds with curtains or valances, or use them alone to cover a window. They come in standard, ready-made sizes, or can be custom-ordered to fit any size or shape window.

The advantage of blinds is that they are adjustable, which makes it easy to control privacy, light, and air. Their disadvantages include a somewhat sterile appearance, unless they are softened with the addition of curtains or valances; the slats, which attract dirt, can be awkward to clean.

OPPOSITE
Simple white shutters let the bold colors in this room take center stage.

RIGHT
This Roman shade incorporates a coordinating fabric pattern into the room's design scheme.

BELOW
Two walls of windows get different treatments in this room. One features simple shutters; the other is an elaborate combination of curtains, matching valance, and shades.

Shades. Generally considered soft window treatments, shades are made of single pieces of fabric or vinyl attached to a roller and operated with a cord or a spring mechanism. Fabric shades can be flat, gathered, or pleated. Some shades can block out the sun entirely when they're drawn; others merely filter it. Use shades alone or with curtains. Like blinds, shades come in standard, ready-made sizes, or they can be custom ordered. Popular variations include Roman shades, balloon shades, pleated-fabric shades, and cellular shades.

The advantages of shades include a versatility of styles and colors and their easy operation in controlling light and privacy. Their disadvantages are that they can be difficult to clean; also, they will not block out sunlight unless they are made of a heavier, more costly room-darkening material.

Shutters. Louvered shutters are made from wood. Open them for air or close them for privacy. They may be painted or stained, and some come with a fabric panel that can be matched to fabric used on other furnishings in the room. Wide louvers have a contemporary appeal; narrow louvers lend a more country feeling. You can purchase standard sizes or custom-order shutters to fit an oddly shaped window.

The advantages of shutters are the privacy they offer when closed and the fact that slats can be opened or closed easily to control air and light. Their disadvantage is that they have to be custom-made for windows that are not of standard dimensions.

Before you shop for any window treatment, consider the room's needs carefully, and walk yourself through the Smart Steps that follow. (See page 89.)

ABOVE
The contemporary wood shutters complement the white window frame and chair rail in this bright bedroom.

LEFT
This half-round window lets sunlight peek into the delightful garden-themed room. A valance and blinds ensure privacy.

OPPOSITE TOP
Striped Roman shades complement the delicate interplay of patterns selected for this bedroom.

OPPOSITE BOTTOM LEFT
Bold tab-top curtain panels match the bedding for a coordinated look that cannot miss.

OPPOSITE BOTTOM RIGHT
A combination of Roman shades and soft curtains in the same fabric tie together a window and French door.

smart steps
window dressing

Step 1 NOTE THE ROOM'S ORIENTATION AND VIEW

Figure out how the room's exposure to the sun throughout the day will affect its function. A nursery may look lovely with the early morning light streaming in, but unless you want baby up at dawn each day, you may need to consider a room-darkening treatment, especially if the window faces east. A west-facing window will get most of its sunlight in the afternoon— just in time for naps—while a southern exposure is bright most of the day. Luckily, most window treatments are adjustable and will allow you to control the amount of light you want to filter into the room at different hours. However, because north-facing windows receive no direct sunlight, window treatments should be adequately lined with insulating material to keep the room temperature comfortable, especially during the chilly winter months.

Step 2 CHOOSE THE PROPER HARDWARE

The right rod, pole, clips, or rings are important for the proper installation of a window treatment because they provide the support. True, some window hardware is decorative, but remember the old adage: form follows function. If you substitute a flimsy metal rod when the installation calls for a substantial wooden pole, the curtains will not hang right. Heavy, highly ornamented finials and rods can look out of place because they are too formal and sophisticated for a young child's room.

Step 3 CHOOSE AN INSIDE OR OUTSIDE MOUNT

You can install your window treatment inside or outside the window opening, depending on whether or not you want the trim to show. However, the time to make this decision is before you shop for curtains and hardware, when you're taking measurements, not after you've begun the installation.

Step 4 MEASURE UP

Even if they're in the same room, two windows can have different measurements. Never assume otherwise. Using a steel measuring tape, carefully take the dimensions of every window in the room.

Step 5 CONSIDER MAINTENANCE

Delicate fabrics and elaborate trims require professional care. You can't throw these materials into the washing machine and dryer. Some custom-made treatments have to be professionally installed and removed as well. Consider your budget carefully if this is an option.

OPPOSITE
Sometimes, it's all in the details. This bluebird shade pull transforms an ordinary roller shade into a one-of-a-kind window treatment. Gingham panels complete the look.

RIGHT
Roman blinds are great not only for the versatility they offer for pattern, color, and texture, but also because they work as well for glass doors as they do for windows.

LEFT
Kids, especially younger ones, spend a lot of time on the floor. A hardwood floor topped with a soft, cushiony rug is a great combination for a play space.

BELOW
This wide-plank hardwood floor in a variegated light stain works perfectly with the country-style furnishings and quilt-patterned bedding.

OPPOSITE
If allergies are a concern, hardwood floors are easy to keep clean and free of dust.

flooring

C hildren of all ages spend a lot of time playing, eating, and sometimes even sleeping on the floor. For these reasons, the flooring material you choose is important. Not only does it need to be comfortable, but also easy to clean.

Innovations in technology have allowed for a wide range of finishes that make the most of style and easy maintenance. As you review these options, remember that some can be mixed and matched to create unique variations within almost any budget. Also review the earlier discussion of color in Chapter 2. If the room is small, a light-color floor will make it feel more spacious; if the room is large, a pattern will add coziness. Of course, you should balance what you decide to put on the floor with the colors and patterns on the other surfaces in the room.

Good flooring is an investment in your child's room that can last through adulthood. Therefore, it's wise to plan carefully.

Wood

Today's manufacturers offer a variety of hardwood flooring. Wood flooring is a traditional favorite, available in strips of 2 to 3 inches wide, or in country-style planks 10 inches wide or more. The look of a parquet floor is unparalleled for its richness of visual texture. Prefinished hardwood tile blocks are now manufactured in a variety of patterns, making parquet possible at a reasonable price.

Softwoods, such as pine and fir, are often used to make simple tongue-and-groove floorboards. Softwoods are less

suitable for high-traffic areas but can survive most kids' rooms well. The hardwoods—maple, birch, oak, or ash—are far less likely to mar with normal use, but a hardwood floor is not indestructible: it will stand up to use, but not abuse.

Both hardwoods and softwoods are graded according to their color, grain, and imperfections. The top of the line is known as clear, followed by select, Number 1 common, and Number 2 common. In addition to budget considerations, the decision to pay top dollar for clear wood or to economize with a lesser grade depends on use factors and design objectives. For example, if you plan to install carpeting or a rug over the wood flooring, the Number 2 common grade is a practical choice. Another factor to use in determining what grade to select is the stain you plan to

use. Imperfections are usually less noticeable with darker stains.

Color stains—reds, blues, and greens—look great in a kid's room where the overall style is casual. Natural wood stains range from very light ash tones to deep, coffee-like colors. Generally, lighter stains make a room feel less formal, and darker, richer stains suggest a traditional atmosphere. Lighter stains—as with lighter colors—create a feeling of openness and make a room look larger; darker stains can make a large, cold space feel warm.

Most wood-flooring installations are handled by professionals, although some kits provide good results and are relatively easy for do-it-yourselfers.

When it comes to maintenance, a regular vacuum cleaning or dust mopping may be all you need if the wood has been sealed properly with polyurethane. You can wash a wood floor as long as you use a product that's manufactured specifically for this purpose. Water and wood generally don't mix well. In most cases, you'll want to keep the flooring soft underfoot by adding a rug or carpeting, which will take the brunt of the abuse and protect little ones from bumps and bruises.

Laminate Products

When your creative side tells you to install wood, but your practical side knows it just won't hold up to your kid's antics, a wood lookalike may be just the solution. Faux wood laminate floors provide you with the look you want but temper it with physical wear and care properties that accommodate kids well. Laminate is particularly suited to children's bedrooms and play-rooms where stain- and scratch-resistance and easy cleanup count. In fact, manufacturers offer warranties against staining, scratching, cracking, and peeling for up to 15 years. To clean laminate, just run the vacuum over it or use a damp mop. You never have to wax these easy-care floors.

The installation of laminate flooring is a reasonably quick and easy do-it-yourself project. You can apply it over virtually any subflooring surface, including wood and concrete. It can also be applied on top of existing ceramic tile, vinyl tile, or vinyl or other sheet flooring. It even works over certain types of carpeting, but check the manufacturer's guidelines before installing.

Vinyl and Other Resilient Flooring

Price, durability, and easy maintenance make resilient flooring an attractive and popular choice for a kid's room. Do-it-yourself installation, an option even for those who are not particularly skilled or experienced, can mean further savings.

Resilient flooring comes in sheet or tile form and in an enormous array of colors and patterns. With tiles, you can

combine color and pattern in limitless ways. Even the sheet form of resilient flooring can be customized with the use of inlay strips, but that's not a do-it-yourself job.

Cushioned sheet vinyl offers the most resilience. It provides excellent stain-resistance; it's comfortable and quiet underfoot; and it's easy to maintain, especially with the attractive no-wax and never-wax finishes that are often available.

Carpeting and Rugs

Carpeting offers an enormous variety of material, style, color, pattern, texture, and cost options. Wool carpeting is the most durable and the most expensive; it also has the advantage of being naturally fire-resistant.

Carpeting made from synthetic fibers offers the greatest variety in terms of color, pattern, and texture; in the short run, it's certainly more affordable. A good compromise would be a wool-synthetic blend, which offers a reasonably wide variety of design options, plus the advantage of some enhanced durability without the expensive pure-wool price tag.

During the manufacturing process, carpet fibers can be woven, tufted, needlepunched, or flocked. Tufted carpet comes in one of three styles: cut pile (suitable for use in any room); loop pile (very durable, especially in high-traffic areas); and cut-and-loop pile (multicolor types of cut-and-loop pile are excellent at hiding soil). In general, woven carpet is the most durable, while flocked carpet is the least durable.

The type of fiber, the density and height of the pile, and the thickness and quality of the yarn are other factors that will affect looks and life span, as will the padding. All of these will affect the price tag, as well.

Area rugs are an excellent device for creating separate play and sleep areas within the room or for dividing the space for sharing. They're also a relatively inexpensive way to add accent colors that help to tie the overall scheme together. However, area rugs should always be backed with a nonskid material. You can hold down small rugs by attaching a hook-and-loop strip to the rug and the floor.

Carpeting and rugs are easy to maintain—vacuum cleaning is all that's required for regular upkeep. Because kids can be tough on any flooring, protect your carpet investment by buying one that is treated at the mill for stain resistance. Periodic cleanings will keep most good-quality carpets fresh for years of use.

OPPOSITE Area rugs offer another opportunity for adding pattern and texture. Use them to protect the floor, provide a cushioned play space, or demarcate room areas.

carpet-stain removal

Always clean up a spot or spill immediately, using white cloths or paper towels. Blot, never rub or scrub, a stain. Work from the outer edge in toward the center of the spot, and then follow up with clean water to remove any of the stain's residue. Blot up any moisture remaining from the cleanup by layering white paper towels over the spot and weighing them down with a heavy object.

- To remove a water-soluble stain, blot as much of it as possible with white paper towels that have been dampened with cold water. If necessary, mix a solution of $\frac{1}{4}$ teaspoon of clear, mild, nonbleach laundry detergent with 32 ounces of water, and then spray it lightly onto the spot. Blot it repeatedly with white paper towels. Rinse it with a spray of clean water; then blot it dry.
- To treat soils made by urine or vomit, mix equal parts of white vinegar and water, and blot the mixture onto the spot with white paper towels; then clean with detergent solution.
- To remove an oil-based stain, blot as much of it as you can; then apply a nonflammable spot remover made specifically for grease, oil, or tar to a clean, white paper towel. Don't apply the remover directly to the carpet, or you may damage the backing. Blot the stain with the treated towel. Wear rubber gloves to protect your hands. Use this method for stains caused by crayons, cosmetics, ink, paint, and shoe polish.
- For spots made by cola, chocolate, or blood, apply a solution of 1 tablespoon of ammonia and 1 cup of water to the stain; then go over it with the detergent solution. Do not use ammonia on a wool carpet. Try an acid stain remover, such as lemon juice or white vinegar diluted with water.
- To remove chewing gum or candle wax, try freezing the spot with ice cubes, and then gently scrape off the gum or wax with a blunt object. Follow this with a vacuuming. If this doesn't work, apply a commercial gum remover to the area, following the manufacturer's directions.

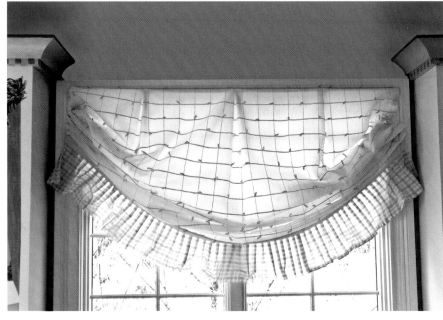

design workbook
THE FAIREST OF THEM ALL

dreams do come true

Picked up from the colors in the Snow White poster, the lime-green fabrics and cool purple color on the walls set a soothing tone for the room.

mirror, mirror

The same fabric used for the draped fabric over the headboard also appears in the delicate ruched window valances. These valances are purely decorative— a way to reinforce the color scheme and coordinate with the comforter colors.

color underfoot

A stain-resistant wall-to-wall carpet, left, is another way to set a room's tone with color. In this room, the bold pink contrasts beautifully with the green walls and bedding and the white furnishings.

design workbook
CHECK IT OUT

party animals

The artist who designed this table and chairs thoughtfully included a smattering of stenciled stars on each seat. Note how the checkerboard design along the table rim and chair backs echoes the pattern of the bears and painted floor "rug."

stars underfoot

A floor stenciled with a galaxy of stars is covered with several layers of clear polyurethane for durability.

soft touch

Having established the checkerboard pattern on the floor and furniture, this valance fabric, top left, repeats the pattern and adds textural interest.

details, details

The checked frame used for this print on the dresser, left, subtly and neatly continues the theme in different colors.

5

decorating the nursery

PLANNING   DESIGN DECISIONS   PULLING TOGETHER A LOOK
DESIGN WORKBOOK

Most expectant parents take a keen interest in decorating baby's first room. Even people who are normally not inclined to care about such matters as curtains and wallpaper want everything to be perfect for their new arrival, right down to the color of the pillowcases. But a newborn is too young to notice the pink ruffle on the crib skirt or the painted bunnies on the wall. To an infant, the nursery is just a place for sleeping, feeding, and diaper changes. That doesn't mean there shouldn't be ruffles or painted bunnies in the room. By all means, decorate the nursery as you would like it, even if your child isn't old enough to appreciate all of your efforts. Know that this is likely to be the only time your design choices won't meet with objections from the peanut gallery. Soon, he will take an important role in these decisions.

LEFT
The nursery is primarily a place for sleeping, so the atmosphere should be tranquil for both the baby and her caregivers.

planning

When you're designing the baby's nursery, one luxurious advantage you have is time. While you are waiting for the baby to arrive, comparison shop for big-ticket items. Get started on some of the work that can be done at your leisure, such as painting and installing wallpaper.

If you're on a tight budget, investigate wholesalers and discounters who may be able to save you money, or wait until certain products go on sale. Consider items that serve more than one purpose, that will grow with your child, or that can be put to use in another room later on. Good investments might include a bassinet that becomes a toy basket, a crib that transforms into a toddler bed (and later still, a regular head- and footboard), or a dresser with a removable changing table on top.

Whatever you choose, just make sure that items you order can be delivered on time. A cradle or bassinet next to your bed is fine—even convenient—for a while. But soon enough, baby is going to outgrow this arrangement and require a sturdy crib in his own separate bedroom.

Also use this time to talk with other parents. They may have good advice to share about products that have worked for them. You can also research ratings for the safety, ease of use, and durability of specific items through organizations such as the National Safety Council and the Juvenile Products Manufacturers' Association. (For more information, see the Resource Guide on page 208.) Another excellent source of information is the Internet. Most manufacturers and retail stores have Web sites, as do the aforementioned organizations, that offer tips about shopping and detailed information.

Just because you do have time, don't squander it. Sometimes just thinking about what needs to be done can paralyze you. On the next page, you'll find tips on where to start.

OPPOSITE TOP
A bath or even a powder room off the nursery is a worthwhile addition if you are considering a remodeling project.

OPPOSITE BOTTOM
Infants find soft textures to be very soothing. Be sure to include a variety of pleasingly touchable fabrics and toys in the crib.

LEFT
To regulate a baby's sleep patterns, consider drapery or shades that allow you to control exactly how much sunlight comes into the room.

smart steps
where to start

Step 1 PICK A LOCATION FOR THE NURSERY

It can be a spare room or a large corner in a room shared by another young child, if necessary. The latter should be a temporary arrangement. An infant will require your attention often, sometimes during the night, and this will disturb your older child's sleep. Ideally, the nursery should be away from the public areas of the house where there's a lot of activity. Don't choose a room that's next to the home office, where there's noise from computers, printers, telephones, and fax machines.

Step 2 MAKE A LIST OF PROJECTS AND TASKS

It could contain everything from adding a room onto the house to simply painting or just buying furniture. If the room needs construction or major renovation, obtain contractors' bids immediately. The earlier you can get the work done, the better. Lots of new materials, such as carpeting and wood products—even some paint—contain noxious chemicals that take time to dissipate. The last thing you want is to expose your newborn's lungs to these fumes.

Step 3 REVIEW YOUR BUDGET

Decide how much you can afford to spend. Buy what you really need first. Skip the cute accessories until you've purchased the necessities.

Step 4 DECIDE ON A LOOK WITH STAYING POWER

Will it be something old-fashioned, modern, plain, or fancy, inspired by a favorite nursery rhyme or bedtime story? Narrow down the field, and then look for furnishings to reinforce your ideas. It's wise to stick with a motif that you can retain through the toddler years and beyond, if possible. That way you won't have to redecorate the room before your child is in kindergarten. If you want to include Babar or Barney, for example, do it with a pillow or some other accessory that can be changed when it becomes too babyish for your maturing child.

design decisions

Every nursery must serve a number of functions. Primarily, it must provide a temperate, safe sleeping area for the baby. A changing and dressing station is also essential. The nursery must accommodate a comfortable rocker, glider, or chair and side table with a lamp where parents can feed or comfort the baby at night. There should be a chest of drawers to store clothing, but a nursery with room left over might also include play space or toy storage. Keep it simple, though. Don't crowd the nursery; just fill it with the essentials and leave enough space on the floor so that there is room for the baby to explore, crawl, and play.

Furnishings will fit into the room in a finite number of configurations, but not all of them are pleasing or practical. Begin by placing the crib. It is likely the largest piece of furniture the room will contain, and it requires some planning for safety. Keep the crib away from windows to avoid drafts and any risk posed by an open window. If one side of the crib will rest against a wall,

keep the area free of wall hangings. Also, make sure the crib is a safe distance from any heating and cooling vent or radiator.

The changing table should be near the door, if possible. That makes it easy to pop in with the baby when necessary. Clean clothes and diapers should be within reach.

Nursery Furnishings

Baby-room decor is about more than cribs and rocking chairs. Little accents that might not cost much can really add to the room's overall appearance. For example, you might consider replacing the existing light-switch cover or changing the knobs on a dresser as two quick fixes for dressing up the room. Should you try to match the nursery's style to the rest of the house? Doing so makes for a cohesive look, but it isn't a mandate that you have to obey. Do what you want. Even if your home is sleek and modern, the nursery can be slightly more traditional to enhance its cozy feeling.

The Crib. If you have to choose where to save a few dollars and where to splurge, invest your money in a good, solid crib. One thing to think about if you're considering a crib that converts to a junior bed (also called a "youth bed") is that you may be using the same mattress, so the sleeping surface really

doesn't get any bigger. Besides, by that time your now potty-training toddler will be delighted to have a real big-boy's bed to go with his new independence. If you decide to go with a convertible crib, make sure the mattress is twin-size.

essential nursery furniture checklist

The nursery calls for basic furniture for the baby's basic needs. Fill in later with those things that you discover will make it easier and more comfortable for you to care for your child.

- ✓ Crib
- ✓ Changing Table
- ✓ Chest of Drawers
- ✓ Comfortable Chair or Rocker
- ✓ Side Table
- ✓ General Lighting
- ✓ Flooring
- ✓ Table Lamp
- ✓ Mobile
- ✓ Baby Monitor

The Consumer Product Safety Commission has issued standards with which all new cribs must comply. If you're reusing an older crib, it may not meet those standards. If the crib is an antique, you may want to consider a reproduction instead.

It's a good idea to check all cribs for safety. Is there any part of the crib—the corner posts for example—that can snag clothing or cause choking? Are there cracks in the finish? Is there a cutout design that could catch baby's arm or neck? Are the rails spaced $2^3/8$ inches apart or less? Does the mattress fill in snugly around the walls of the crib? You should not be able to fit two fingers between the mattress and the side of the crib.

A crib should be adjustable to three or four different mattress heights to accommodate baby as she grows. Also, it has to be solid. Give it a good shake to make sure that there are no missing screws or loose joints, slats, or knobs. As baby gets stronger, she will jump in the crib, so you don't want to risk a collapse. Any crib must be easy to operate. Lift and lower the rails. Try doing this with one hand because there are times when you'll have to lower the rail while holding the baby with one arm.

The Changing Table. You'll be changing diapers for two to three years, so make sure you buy the right changing table. Look for one with guardrails and safety straps. You'll also need a place

to store diapers, lotion, cloth towels, and clothes within arm's reach. Some changing tables feature shelves underneath, but that means you'll have to bend over to get what you need, which takes your eyes and hands off the baby. A shelf installed on the wall above the table is a better idea. You could use a portable crib on top of a dresser as a changing station as well. When you don't need it anymore, just remove the crib, and the dresser is ready for a hutch or a mirror.

If you can, purchase a changing table that lets the baby face you as you change him; it's a more comfortable position for you and baby. See the illustration on page 104, which shows an example of an efficient changing station for the nursery. The table is the central design element.

A Dresser. Sometimes parents postpone large furniture purchases until a child is little older. In that case, a hand-me-down chest or dresser is fine because you'll still need a place to store the baby's clothes. Just make sure that the finish isn't chipping and that the joints are solid. Pull out the drawers to make sure they don't stick. If they do, lubricate the runners. (Refer to "Good Furniture Construction," on page 62 in Chapter 3, for more tips.)

If you're buying something new, don't choose anything without inspecting it carefully; sometimes manufacturers cut back, making the face of the drawer deeper than the actual depth of the drawer. Drawers have to be roomy in order to accommodate the storage needs of your child as she grows. One sweatshirt that fits an average-size sixth-grader fits into the same space as a stack of four infant-size clothing items.

A Chair. A nursery really needs a rocker or glider. Because this is where you'll sit while feeding or just holding the baby, it should be comfortable for your body. Shop for something that will support your lower back. A chair that you use with a newborn will last throughout childhood and into adulthood if it is well-constructed. Look for one with padded cushions covered in an easy-care, stain-resistant fabric.

Lighting. Recessed or ceiling-mounted lighting provides general illumination for any room. Whatever ambient light source you choose for the nursery, be sure to install it on a dimmer so that you can lower the light level when baby sleeps. Most people also use a table lamp beside the nursing chair. Another option, one that will prove safer when your baby becomes mobile, is a wall-mounted fixture. Because babies are attracted to light sources, choose fixtures that will shade baby's eyes from the glare of a bare bulb. And never install a lamp within baby's reach. (For specific tips on lighting, see page 68 in Chapter 3.)

Flooring. The most logical choices, hardwood, laminate, and resilient flooring, are all fine materials for a nursery floor. Children spend a lot of time on the floor and tend to spill all sorts of things. Few parents will go out of their way to install a hardwood floor solely in a nursery, but should it already exist in the room, it's not a bad performer. A polyurethane-sealed wood floor requires minimal care. A simple vacuuming and occasional dust-mopping is all that is needed to keep wood, laminate, or resilient flooring clean. Because they are not unyieldingly hard surfaces, as are stone or ceramic tile, they don't pose much danger for those first tentative steps—unless they are polished to a high-gloss finish. An area rug that has a nonskid backing will make such a floor relatively risk-free for playing.

If your budget is tight, you could treat an old wood floor to an artful painted finish. Try stripes or a stenciled pattern. Another money-saving creative solution is a painted canvas floor-cloth. All you need is a pattern, easy-to-work-with acrylic paints, a stencil brush, and disposable foam brushes. You can find these materials and instructions at any craft store.

Carpeting, on the other hand, muffles noise and lends warmth, especially in areas where drafts are a problem. Falls are naturally cushioned and tentative walkers tend to do well on a carpeted surface. But wall-to-wall carpeting can be expensive, especially when it is a high-quality wool or wool blend, and can harbor dust mites, pollen, and other irritants for the allergy-prone. If you choose carpeting and expect it to last through the years, select one that is stain-resistant and neutral in color so that your choices for other surfaces aren't limited when you're ready to make a change in the future.

Accessories. Most are optional, but a mobile over the crib and a baby monitor are practically essential. Because newborns are more sensitive to movement and sound than some other stimuli, such as color, mobiles are very appealing, especially those that play tunes. A reliable baby monitor lets you hear your baby when you're out of the room. Make sure these items meet the standards of the Juvenile Products Manufacturers Association.

LEFT
By setting the cribs into drapery coronets, the room is already set for the twin beds these siblings will eventually need.

RIGHT
A cozy window seat is perfect for sharing a story or watching the world go by together.

smart tip PASS IT ON

The best way to save money on nursery furnishings is to accept gifts from other new mothers, says interior designer Coral M. Nalfie. Many parents are happy to pass along things that their baby has outgrown or doesn't need anymore. If you have a friend or relative with a baby 3 to 6 months older than yours, they'll be the perfect one to ask.

Garage sales, flea markets, and consignment stores are a great place to buy slightly used pieces. You'll be able to save a lot of money compared to a new retail purchase and maybe even have higher quality than you'd get otherwise. And don't just look at baby items, Nalfie suggests. You might see a great chest of drawers or an antique rocking chair that, with a fresh coat of paint, would be perfect for the nursery.

pulling together a look

Some parents envision a bright, cheerful place where baby will be stimulated by a variety of colorful shapes and forms. Other moms and dads have something more subtle in mind. Although it is true that a baby's eyesight gradu- ally develops over the first six months of life, it's never too soon to include simple patterns and shapes near the crib and changing table. You can accomplish this with linens, mobiles, and soft wall art that will attract a newborn who has a fairly well-developed visual sense. Stick to simple geometric shapes that are easier for baby to recognize. While wallpaper, curtains, and other accessories can pull together a look or theme for the room, baby won't really take much notice of these.

Color is always a personal choice. Although some child-development experts believe that sharp contrasts, such as the pairing of black and white, stimulate newborns, they also acknowledge that primary colors (red, blue, and yellow) are

recognized by babies in the earliest months as well. Still other studies suggest that babies gaze longest at yellow, white, pink, and red. None of this information is conclusive. And there is no evidence to suggest that any particular color is harmful. The best advice is to go with the colors that most please you.

Theme Decorating

A common device used in children's rooms is theme decorating. This involves repeating one motif throughout the room. It can be anything from a simple graphic, to a fairy tale, to a cartoon or nursery-rhyme character. This is really an easy way out if you're stumped for time or inspiration. You can find wallpapers and borders, curtains, and linens that feature some popular themes, but be prepared to make changes once your little one develops a mind of his own. Painted murals are another way to do this, often uniquely. But this can be time consuming and difficult, so unless you're a skilled artist, you'll have to hire professional help. This can be considerably more costly than hanging wallpaper, but the effect may be worth the expenditure.

On the other hand, you don't have to decorate with a theme. Some of the most beautiful, classic nursery designs rely simply on traditional decorating elements and a pleasing interplay of color, pattern, and texture. Frankly, if you want to get longevity out of your design, this is the way to go.

Theme Alternatives

Approach the nursery as you would any bedroom. This will make it easier for you to incorporate the interests of your toddler later. Floral, plaid, and geometric designs can all work as harmoniously in a baby's room as in any other bedroom. You can give the room a formal air with lace window dressings or a cozy, casual feeling with rich, flannel-checked accessories. Besides, if you keep things simple, you can always add a wallpaper border, new window treatments, or a bed set with a motif that your child chooses on her own once she's old enough.

OPPOSITE
A distinctive, round crib with a canopy makes baby's bed the focal point of this pretty room.

ABOVE
A wallpaper border is an easy way to incorporate a nursery rhyme or favorite motif into the design scheme.

Gender-Neutral Design. This type of approach is all about preference. Certainly, you can use flowers in a boy's room or a jungle theme in a girl's room. And research shows that women's favorite colors are nearly identical to men's. So where did this custom of pink for girls and blue for boys come from? Look at it this way: you can be an iconoclast, a traditionalist, or you can avoid the conflict altogether by designing the nursery to reflect a gender-neutral theme.

There are lots of colors and motifs that are not gender-specific; stick to them if you're in doubt. Gingham checks, stripes, plaids, and solids in bright, lively colors will work better than floral prints. As for decorating motifs, the sun, moon, and stars are a safe choice, and although space exploration and solar system designs used to carry boyish overtones, with heroes like Sally Ride to admire, it's a perfectly appropriate motif for any child's room. Baby animals are equally associated with either gender, but hearts

LEFT
Meticulously hand-painted furnishings and the coordinated fabric that inspired them make this a one-of-a-kind nursery.

RIGHT
To find the best-looking accessories, don't forget the toy box. Kids' stuff is designed to be colorful and frequently looks great on display.

will somehow always imply "girl." Nursery rhymes and fairy tales are good choices, especially if both a boy and a girl are the main characters—as in Hansel and Gretel or Jack and Jill. That's one way to avoid gender stereotyping.

Finishing Touches

After the wallpapering and painting is done, the curtains are up, and the furniture is placed, it's time to give the room its finishing touches. If you've exhausted your budget, don't worry: you can accessorize charmingly with the baby's belongings. Who hasn't smiled with delight at the sight of cute little baby shoes and those tiny little first outfits? Hang them in full view from a Shaker-style pegged rack. Display charming baby quilts or blankets that you received as gifts simply by draping them over the chair. Use inexpensive but pretty ribbon as a tieback to dress up plain curtains, or glue it to the edges of a plain lampshade.

Precut stencils, stamps, and blocks, available at craft stores, let you customize everything in the room, from furniture to fabric. Just keep the stencil flat against the surface you are decorating and offload excess paint. You need a separate brush for each color you use; blot paint into cut-out areas, don't brush it on. Be sure to clean the stencil between applications.

Stamps are even easier to use. Simply load the block with paint, blot, and then stamp the raised design onto the surface.

safety in the nursery

It's not difficult to make your newborn's room a safe environment. After all, a baby spends most of his time either in the crib or in your arms. But babies grow fast, becoming more independent with each day. Because your child will be a busy toddler before you know it, you may want to think ahead and get the room ready for the age of exploration. Here's a checklist that will help you child-proof the room for a young baby.

- Install outlet caps and covers on all electrical outlets.
- Play it safe with electrical cords. Don't run them under the carpet, and don't let them dangle from a tabletop or dresser.
- Use only blinds and shades without looped cords.
- Your baby's ability to pull herself up on the crib rails will likely coincide with her teething schedule. To protect her from swallowing paint or varnish chips, install snap-on crib rail protectors.
- Install childproof locks on drawers and cabinets.
- Tack down carpets.
- Keep the crib far enough away from any window so that the baby can't grab any cords or curtains, or try to climb out the window.
- Remove small objects and toys with small parts that the baby might swallow.
- Make sure furniture is assembled properly. Check for loose nuts and bolts.
- Hang a mobile out of the reach of the baby. Once the baby can stand, remove the mobile to ensure his safety.
- Keep the side rails up at all times when the baby is in the crib.
- Install a smoke alarm in the room.
- Use a monitor to listen to the baby when you're away from the room.
- Follow the recommendations of the Consumer Product Safety Commission regarding cribs.

design workbook
SOFT SANCTUARY

light and airy

Gleaming white-painted furniture combines with the room's wood trim to provide a clean contrast to the gentle yellow walls.

playful curves

The whimsically styled dresser, top left, features delicately carved drawer panels and legs that echo the styling of the crib and shelving.

blue notes

Fabrics bring an ethereal shade of blue into the mix. Used as a crib surround, the drapery, left, shields baby from the light that streams in from the sunny windows.

now and later

A large area rug muffles footsteps and will later provide a cushiony place to play.

design workbook

ADORNED WITH LOVE

goodnight moon

A stenciled wall over the crib gives baby a starry view every night. Stenciling is easy to accomplish and yields a professional look.

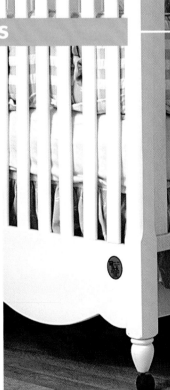

just my height

Low-placed shelves keep favorite toys within safe reach. Ordinary furnishings look special when painted with one-of-a-kind details. (See also top left.)

tiny posies

Decorated with wildflowers and gentle creatures, these unmatched drawers and dresser become unforgettable with these hand-painted details. (See also left and far left.)

6
designs toddlers will love

 toddler, even a very young one, forms an attachment to his room and clearly understands it to be his own. He knows his clothes belong in the room, his toys live there, and every night his room is where he goes to sleep. His room is also likely to be the only one in the house where he is allowed to touch most of what he sees. So it's important to plan a room that not only pleases your child's senses but also serves his needs. This is a period of transition, from totally dependent baby to ever-more independent tot. It's the time for moving from crib to bed, for acquiring possessions, and for developing play skills. In addition to the decorative elements you choose for the room, there are other important factors that should be in your game plan: buying a bed, determining storage needs, planning play space, and making the room safe.

LEFT
Brightly painted rollout bins are a smart and attractive solution to the inevitable challenge of toy storage.

By the age of two, your child will demonstrate numerous likes and dislikes. You may be able to discern some of her preferences for specific colors and favorite themes by the toys she gets most excited about or particular articles of clothing she likes more than others. Although it's too early to assume that these favorites will last, you can use them as clues to help you design a room that reflects her personality and stimulates her imagination.

The transition from nursery to big boy's room can be a little disruptive for a toddler, even with his growing sense of independence. To counter any fears brought on by the change, get your child accustomed to the idea gradually. Here's what you can do to prepare your youngster for the changes ahead.

smart steps
getting started

Step 1 COMMUNICATE
It's never too soon to start talking to your child. Explain that this is her room. Parents of toddler-age children have heard the word "mine" often enough to know that the promise of "ownership" is enticing to very young children.

Step 2 INVOLVE YOUR CHILD
Let your tot "help" you by bringing some of his things into the room, for example. Show him where his toys and clothes will go and ask him to put them away.

Step 3 APPEAL TO HER PRIDE
Emphasize that because she's not a baby anymore, she's going to sleep in a grownup bed now, and she'll have "big girl" furniture.

LEFT
This cubby system holds a nearly endless supply of the small treasures that children naturally accumulate.

ABOVE
At a very young age, a beloved rag doll might inspire the direction of your child's room design.

OPPOSITE
If the space is large enough, you might be able to accommodate a play area within the bedroom.

a room plan

Room to play is probably the most important thing you can provide to young children. Kids of this active age need rocking horses and indoor gym sets. If space permits, divide the room into separate zones for sleeping, story-telling, crafts, and playing. You may be able to contain some of the mess if finger paints are permitted only at the crafts table (where snacks may be taken, too), and toys remain only in the play zone. You can help this idea along by visually partitioning the space with different flooring types, such as carpeting near the bed, wood or a wood-laminate in the play zone, and resilient or vinyl flooring in the craft area.

Tight on space? Arrange all the furniture against the walls to free up more floor area for playing in the center of the room. Look around the room and decide what you don't need to keep. If floor space is limited, don't include a chair and side table in the plan for the time being. (You can always sit next to your child in bed when you read to him.)

Furnishings

If your crib converts to a toddler bed, you're in good shape, because the nursery dresser will likely suffice for the time being as well. However, it's probably more practical to buy an adult-size bed at this stage. With the addition of a child's table-and-chair set and storage for toys, these items may be able to carry you and your little one through until she is about 5 or 6 years old.

The Bed. A twin-size adult bed is ideal, although you may have to buy a double bed somewhere down the line as your child gets older and wants to have friends for sleepovers. For a young toddler who is adjusting to a grownup bed, there are twin beds that come with guard rails that can be removed later. Why not a toddler bed? First, it may not have guard rails, although it is lower to the floor. Plus, a toddler bed is seldom constructed with box springs, which means it cannot provide the proper support your child needs. Shop for a twin mattress with at least 200 coils or a double-size that has at least 300 coils.

If you don't want to commit to a specific furniture style now, simply buy the twin-size frame, mattress, and box spring. A headboard and a footboard are optional items and can be added later if you want to coordinate the bed with other furniture in the room. Otherwise, something improvised, such as a stenciled design on the wall behind the bed, can be changed easily when your child outgrows it later.

Well-constructed novelty beds can serve well, and may be passed from one child to the next. Although some youngsters may want a bed that's not childlike in a couple of years, novelty beds remain popular with most children until age 8 or 10.

Storage. One dresser is probably sufficient for a child this young. Pass on the dresser mirror for the time being, or just put it in storage. Things tend to get thrown around young children's rooms, and a large mirror that can shatter is a potential disaster. Install one later when you feel your child is ready.

If you are considering more furniture at this time, clean-lined designs that work with a variety of decorating styles are best. Beds with built-in storage are particularly practical. Furniture that is designed specifically for kids and has met the

standards set forth by the Juvenile Products Manufacturers Association and the Consumer Products Safety Commission can be considered risk-free. But if you're looking at furniture designed for adults, take into consideration ornate woodwork that can cause injury by catching little arms and legs, plus any design elements that may present choking hazards.

What's most important is to create storage for all of the toys that start to accumulate at this age. When your tot gets tired of a favorite game, toy, or stuffed animal, put it away in the attic, garage, or basement for a while and bring out a different toy, so that the play choices always seem fresh to your child.

essential furnishings checklist

This may be the time to start furnishing the room for real. You don't have to do it all at once. Here's a list of items that should serve as a guideline for planning your budget.

- ✓ Bed
- ✓ Chest of Drawers
- ✓ Toy Box
- ✓ Small Table and Chairs
- ✓ Extra Seating
- ✓ Nightstand
- ✓ Lighting Fixtures
- ✓ Flooring

OPPOSITE
The guardrails on this bed can be removed when your child outgrows them. If you are using a standard bed, you can use guardrails that are inserted between the box spring and mattress.

TOP
This seaworthy bed accommodates an entire crew of furry friends and makes an exciting focal point in this nautical-theme bedroom.

LEFT
Make certain your tot's toy box is fitted with safety hinges to protect tiny fingers from injury. Even with protective hinges, avoid a toy box with a very heavy lid.

Crates, cubbies, and plastic bins provide excellent toy storage. Kids get out of bed at night, and they can trip over objects left on the floor. Bins on wheels are handy for clean up at the end of the day. Although a traditional toy box is useful, make sure it operates with safety hinges. It's fine to use an old trunk or box that wasn't intended for toys, as long as you retrofit it with the proper protective hinges.

Shelves are great for toy storage. However, if your child is a climber, shelves can offer an invitation to dangerous exploration. On the other hand, if you keep shelves low enough on the wall for your child to reach, you're helping him learn to pick up after himself.

Adjustable shelves that rest on supports attached to wall-mounted steel brackets offer the most flexibility. Otherwise, plastic crates used as cubbies may be affixed to the walls for storage. Anything heavy that has the potential to tip over, such as tall bookcases or storage compartments, should be bolted securely to the walls.

For bulkier items such as bedding, coats, and jackets, install a closet organizer. Easy-to-assemble, wire-coated systems come in numerous configurations and include bins, baskets, drawers, and shelves. Lower hanging rods make it possible for kids to begin putting away their things, as do children's clothes trees and pegged racks.

There is another option: custom-built storage, which will serve your child's needs for years to come. It's a good investment, particularly in a small room that defies organization. If you hire a professional installer, explain that you expect the pieces to accommodate your child's storage needs now (stuffed animals, storybooks, toys) and in the future (heavy textbooks, a DVD collection, perhaps a TV). Don't forget to get references and check them out. Then obtain several estimates for the work.

Small Table and Chairs. A tot-sized table-and-chair set provides a spot for fantasy and creativity. Since little ones like to get their fingers into things, this is where they can safely play with paints, crayons, clay, and other messy items. It can be a place for light snacks and teddy bear tea parties, too. Sturdy plastic sets can take a real beating, and they can be scrubbed down without causing harm. You can buy a set made of wood, too, or look for an unfinished table and chairs that you can customize with paints. Use a semigloss paint, which can be wiped clean with a damp sponge.

Lighting. Lighting requirements change as children grow. At this stage, you'll need fixtures that spread light evenly around the room, as well as a night light that can be left on for the many times you will check on your little one. You'll also need a reading lamp for storybook time. It can be near the bed or next to a chair, wherever you'll sit while reading. Task lighting for toddlers isn't necessary, because they're still too young for crafts and homework.

For good general lighting, install recessed or ceiling-mounted fixtures on a dimmer switch. A table lamp can be a risky choice because it can be knocked down when small children become rambunctious. And running kids can trip on cords. Instead, consider a wall-mounted fixture or sconce with a light source you can direct. Whatever you choose, never put a lamp where a youngster can get burned by a hot bulb.

Flooring. Just as in a nursery, flooring for a toddler's room should be chosen with practicality in mind. Little ones spend a lot of time playing on the floor, and they spill stuff. You'll need a surface that can stand up to toys that are dragged from one end of the room to the other, and that can be swept and mopped easily. That makes resilient flooring or a laminate product the most suitable choices. Wood, especially if it has been sealed with polyurethane, is easy to keep clean. However, it may scratch, depending on the finish. If you want wood to retain its good looks, invest in a finish that can be damp mopped. For warmth underfoot, install an area rug with a skid-proof backing by the bed. Choose something you can pop into the washing machine If the area rug is large, regular vacuuming will suffice.

Carpeting is another option. But because it is not as easy to keep clean as other types of flooring, it may be better suited to an older child's room. Carpeting may also pose a problem for children with allergies and asthma because it can harbor dust and other allergens, making regular daily vacuuming a must.

OPPOSITE TOP
Some beds are sold with rolling bins that can be accessed easily by little ones. You can fill them with toys, clothes, or favorite storybooks.

OPPOSITE BOTTOM
Five banks of storage bins stacked along a wall add a custom look to this child's room. The stenciled alphabet provides good practice for preschoolers.

ABOVE
Storing pretty things in plain sight, such as a little girl's frilly dress and shoe collection, establishes this room's unique personality.

smart tip

SOFT LANDINGS

Kids naturally gravitate to the floor when they play, so it's a smart idea to provide some cushioning and warmth. Find one or two area rugs that you can toss into the wash from time to time. Interlocking foam mats are also easy to keep clean and provide a smooth, even surface for building blocks and wheeled vehicles.

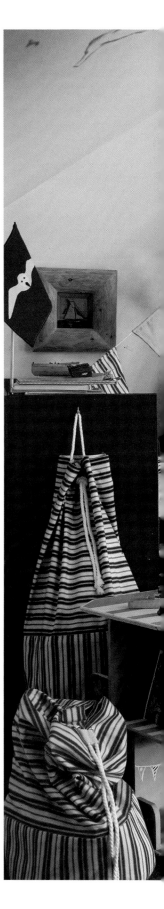

decorating for toddlers

lthough your child is no longer a baby, themes carried over from the nursery may still suitable. Depending on your original choices, you may not need to change the wall and floor treatments at all. Babyish designs will become inappropriate by the end of the toddler stage, but other themes may last until school age.

If you're decorating a room from scratch, however, a good place to begin is with color. At this stage, asking your child to choose a favorite is probably futile. She may give you an answer, but it's likely to change every time you ask. Reliable studies indi-

ABOVE
Young children are attracted to bright colors. Keep this in mind when buying or crafting accessories for their rooms.

RIGHT
The sail on this nautical bed provides a bright focal point and accentuates the room's peaked roofline.

smart tip

CUTE BEDS

A well-constructed novelty bed, such as a "racing car," can be as decorative as it is practical. If it is not too juvenile, it can remain a favorite for years.

cate that bright colors attract toddler-age children, with red and yellow the standout favorites. In general, bold colors are stimulating, while cool colors have a relaxing effect. You may want to experiment with the effect of various colors on your child. Try out a lively scheme if you think your child could benefit from more stimulation. Conversely, see what happens to your overly energetic tot in a room decorated with quiet, soft colors.

Pastels appear to be less appealing to toddlers than bright hues, but that doesn't mean you have to replace them if they already exist in the room. You can easily make a change with a wallpaper border or new curtains, for example. But you're not going to do any harm by sticking with what you have. If you decide to make changes, go with geometric prints, stripes, plaids, or any other classic motif that isn't too childish. That way the wallcoverings, curtains, and bed linens will last well into the school years or until your son or daughter grows tired of them.

Because young children are more attracted by color than form, color is an excellent way to get your child excited about a new room. If you dislike bright or primary colors, choose a neutral scheme and accent it with bright red, blue, or yellow, or a combination of all three. So many toys and accessories designed for children of this age are manufactured in these colors, and that will make accessorizing the room a breeze.

Another approach is to experiment with various tints and shades of one primary color to find attractive variations on a monochromatic (one-color) scheme. For example, try using different shades of blue for the walls, trim, window treatment, and bed linens. Then, if you or your child grows tired of this color later, you can simply replace one element, such as the walls or curtains, with a pleasing new hue.

Two or More to a Room

It's quite common for two young siblings to share a room. If the co-occupants are around the same age, the arrangement can be fairly easy. Each child should have a separate bed, but an activity table and the play space can be shared. It's a good idea to provide separate toy storage for each youngster, but this can be as simple as assigning one toy box or shelf to each child. A bedside table at this age is not necessary, but it always comes in handy—even if it's just for a night light. For a symmetrical look, one shared table between twin beds is fine. Chairs or futons that convert to twin beds are another space-saving option. Look into beds that come with under-bed storage drawers.

A school-age child sharing a room with a much younger brother or sister is a more difficult, but sometimes unavoidable situation. Both children need their own separate area in the room. You also must provide storage for the older child that the toddler cannot access for his own safety. Share with your older child the job of seeing that dangerous items such as scissors, pencils, and very small toys are kept out of their sibling's reach. However, it is not appropriate to expect your older child to have complete responsibility for the safety of a younger sibling.

When there is a substantial age difference between the room's occupants, avoid a decorating theme that is too juvenile. Keep the motif neutral by skipping wallpaper or fabrics with cartoon characters or other childish themes. Instead, select something that would be appropriate for any age, such as a floral print in a room shared by girls or plaid for a boys' room. Or paint the walls a solid color instead. You can use accessories, such as a night light, soft wall art, and a few stuffed animals for the younger child's half of the room; then let your older child hang posters or prints on her side of the space.

Furniture that divides the room is a good idea if there is enough space for modular pieces. Otherwise, a folding screen will give your older child some privacy. If necessary, this can be folded up during the day to allow light from windows on one wall to fill the entire room.

You can also divide the space in half visually by choosing two different themes. For example, if it's a boys' room, decorate with a baseball theme on one side and a hockey theme on the other. Individual themes for two girls might be dance and gymnastics. Or you could decorate with two totally different motifs that have been selected by each child. Use complementary color schemes to unify the two areas while providing visual separation.

safety in the toddler's room

Toddlers seem to have a sixth sense that draws them like magnets to potential sources of danger. It's really just their natural curiosity and growing independence. Here's a list of things that you can do to keep them free from harm.

- Install caps and covers on all electrical outlets.
- Use window guards that restrict the size and access of window openings.
- Tie or wrap up long cords on blinds and shades so that they are out of reach and there are no loops.
- Use molded plastic electrical cord covers.
- Install devices in place of your switch-plate covers that lower the switch to a child's level.
- Remove lamps completely unless they are safely out of reach.
- Secure heavy furniture to the wall with bolts or with straps and brackets.
- Keep toys off the floor at night.
- Use small slide locks placed out of reach to prevent opening and closing of bifold doors that can catch fingers.
- Keep conventional doors from closing with foam doorstops that fit over the top of the door.
- Install doorknobs without locks.
- Use bed rails.
- Don't place furniture directly under a window.
- Use a toy chest with safety hinges.
- Don't put a toy on top of a high shelf or dresser. Make the toy accessible if it's going to be in view.
- Discard anything with small parts.

LEFT
The deep-hued walls in this room are punctuated by decoratively hung quilts, striped bed linens, and the scrollwork on the metal bedframes.

Finishing Touches

Although you might feel tempted, refrain from adding too many accessories to a young child's room. This is especially true when it comes to delicate or small objects. The point is to make the space a carefree zone, where everything is touchable and safe. For example, because lower parts of walls traditionally take a beating from toddlers armed with crayons, chalk, and markers, don't fight it. Instead, mask off a section, and paint it with chalkboard paint. This is a latex-based product that you can paint over later when you're ready to redecorate the room. Using chalk, little kids can draw and practice writing their ABCs to their hearts' delight. Plus, their scrawls and scribbles will be erasable, so they can draw new masterpieces again and again. Store-bought formulas of chalkboard paint are available in traditional green and black. But it is also possible to mix your own shade by adding two tablespoons of unsanded tile grout to one cup of flat latex paint. In addition to walls, this mixture can be used to create a tabletop drawing surface or to decorate doors.

Another way to pack the room with personality is with decorative paint effects. What's more, sponged or ragged finishes camouflage smudge marks and greasy fingerprints, and the walls can be painted over when it is time to update the look of the room. If you are looking for an easy project, try a peaceful painted sky. Apply sky-blue paint over a white base coat. After it dries, slap white paint over the surface using a 4-inch-wide decorator brush. Working at a 45-degree angle and making short, random strokes, pull the paint out until it is thin in some areas. Overlay the paint in places for uneven color. Use a 2-inch-wide brush tipped in white paint to make clouds.

LEFT
A painted mural can bring beloved book characters to life and provide a decorating focal point. Once your child outgrows the theme, it can be easily covered with paint.

OPPOSITE
Closet organizing systems can divide a large closet into manageable sections, making it easy to store specific types of items.

smart tip NEAT STORAGE

A well-organized closet not only makes getting dressed easier but also helps teach your child
to be orderly and to begin to take responsibility for his wardrobe and personal possessions.

design workbook

SUGAR AND SPICE

storybook friends

This all-white room gets a color lift from painted murals illustrating classic children's fairytales. (See also bottom right.)

viva la france

The white-washed floor and antique iron bed give this room an innocent, romantic look.

just for me

Two tot-sized armchairs make it clear just who lives in this room. A mom-sized chair, top left, provides the perfect perch for reading bed-time stories.

open sesame

A Dutch door with glass panes, far left, is an unusual feature that adds to the sunlit charm of this room.

design workbook

RED, YELLOW, AND BLUE

primarily cheery

A bright yellow and red comforter combined with the blue of the chair and rug features all the primary colors in this cheerful space.

gym dandy

A play space adjoining a home gym, top left, allows parents to keep a watchful eye while working out.

on the grow

Items from the nursery, such as the rocker, mobile, and bedside lamp, right, still work well in this toddler's busy world.

bold bath

This bath, left, uses the primary color trio in the shower curtains, wall color, and rugs. All can easily be changed as children get older.

7

expanding
young horizons

ORGANIZING IDEAS   A ROOM PLAN   DECORATING
DESIGN WORKBOOK

Primary school children between the ages of 6 and 11 are

definitely ready to tell you what they want in a bedroom. Along with their

developing sense of self comes a need to imagine the world through their

own eyes, in a manner that might be different from your perspective.

Don't be surprised if your second grader complains that her old room is

"babyish." Struggling for independence, and yet acutely sensitive to peer

pressure and the influences of TV and other media, she may even

surprise you with her sophisticated ideas.

At this stage, children also begin to think critically. They know what

they like. With good communication, you and your

child can devise a plan for the room together. Play

space is still necessary, but a place for doing home-

work and other projects is more important now.

LEFT
Built-in beds
resemble adven-
turers' safari
bunks. Vintage
suitcases enhance
the fantasy and
provide storage.

By the age that children begin to work on nightly homework assignments, many parents want to incorporate a computer station into the bedroom. This is also the time to replace a toddler bed with something more adult, if you haven't already done so. School-age kids are forging friendships, and love sleepovers and slumber parties. If the room is too small for an extra bed, a trundle is an excellent solution. These are also key acquisition years—there are more toys, clothes, sports equipment, electronic games, you name it. In this chapter, you'll find ideas for storage and other ways to keep the room neat.

organizing ideas

Your child is now old enough to be involved in some of the renovation process. Depending on his personality and interests, he may want to participate in decisions such as color choices and furniture styles. Of course, what he may not understand is that certain things he thinks are "cool" now are impractical, and he may tire of them sooner than he realizes. Although it may be hard to convince him, you can offer compromises to any fad-inspired or unusual requests.

Most kids have lots of ideas. Listen to them. Write them down. If she can't be specific about what she likes, show her pictures in magazines. Talk to her about her friends' rooms. Find out what she doesn't like about her existing bedroom. Avoid leading questions. The idea is to find out what pleases your child, not to coax her into pleasing you. To get a conversation going with your child about her room's decor, follow these suggestions.

smart steps
design dialogue

■ Step 1 TALK ABOUT COLOR
The makers of children's toys and clothing know how to pick colors that kids will like. There are always the traditional favorites, but you'll also notice certain color trends if you browse through a kids' clothing store. Ask your youngster to pick out the colors that he likes. Make a note of them. Try this again in a few days to see if he's consistent in his selections. If so, you've got a color with which to work. If it's something that's too trendy or unconventional for your taste, try using it as an accent color or for accessories such as the curtains or bed linens. That way, you can please your child and then change the items when they become tiresome or appear outdated.

■ Step 2 DISCUSS THEMES OR PATTERNS
Your child may be too young to think in abstract terms, so ask her what kind of room she imagines. If she says she'd like an old-fashioned dollhouse, maybe a Victorian theme is the way to go. If her fantasy looks more like outer space, perhaps a sun, moon, and stars theme is in order. Use the clues your child gives you to direct your choices for some of the room's elements, such as a wallpaper pattern or a style of furniture. You might even be able to show her various options. Take home samples from the wallpaper or fabric store that you can look at together.

■ Step 3 MAKE A LIST OF THINGS THAT WILL GO INTO THE ROOM
Besides the obvious—a bed, a chest of drawers—there are other furnishings and items that you and your youngster may want to keep in the room. If it will be something large, such as a fish tank, you'll have to account for it in your floor plan. A hobby table, storage for arts and crafts, a ballet bar, a train set, or other space-consuming items must be measured and accounted for, but you can veto some things that may be better stored elsewhere. For example, sports equipment should go in the garage, and a noisy nocturnal hamster may be kept in a cage in the family room or the playroom.

■ Step 4 NARROW DOWN THE FIELD
You can't leave the entire decision up to a child, no matter how much you want to encourage creativity and participation. Some choices are just too complicated for a kid to make. Mixing patterns and color schemes should be guided by a mature eye. When it comes to selecting a bed or desk, rely on your own better judgment with regard to size, durability, versatility, and affordability. It's a lot easier to change a quilt than it is to replace an expensive piece of furniture.

ABOVE
As a child matures, the activities that take place in the room must adapt to her changing needs and interests.
Space for studying and practicing becomes more important, as does a place for personal grooming.

a room plan

At this point it's a good idea to refer back to Chapter 1 to review the section entitled "Evaluating the Space," which begins on page 15. If you haven't already fully furnished the room, you'll have to do it now. Drawing up a floor plan will let you work with different layouts until you find the best one for the space. Experiment with a new room arrangement that reflects your child's needs at this time. If you are adding a computer to the room, locate the desk where the monitor will not reflect light from a nearby window (or plan on installing the prop-

er adjustable window treatment). Remember, the glare from natural light, or even an artificial source, can cause eyestrain. Give thought to mirror placement as well the location of a TV screen, if you are allowing one in the bedroom. Glass reflects light. For optimum TV viewing, the distance between the monitor and the seating (typically, the bed) should be three times the size of the screen. Make sure to note electrical outlets on your plan as well.

A drawing of the space will also help you judge the suitability of various pieces of furniture with regard to scale and proportion. As your child matures, he'll have increasing needs for storage and display. He may want a larger bed or more room to do school projects. Modular furniture pieces are a good idea because you can buy what you need and arrange them accord-

TOP LEFT AND LEFT
The key to mixing patterns such as these gingham checks and the floral curtains is to match the intensity of the color.

ABOVE
Everything's coming up roses for the sisters who share this lovely room, decorated in a variety of vintage floral patterns.

ingly. Don't forget that the unused space under the bed is excellent for storage, too. Under-bed drawers or plastic containers that slide under the box spring can hold anything from socks and pajamas to school papers. When floor space is tight, you can add more closed or open storage with shelves. Bins, baskets, and boxes can store things that you don't want on display out of sight. Converting an old toy chest into storage for all those bulky items, such as sweaters, extra quilts and blankets, and out-of-season clothing is a smart idea, too. Repaint or cover the chest with leftover wallpaper to create a charming piece that coordinates with the rest of the room's decor.

While it's true that today's children are taller than their ancestors were at the same age, most kids are still shorter than the average adult. Keep that in mind when you're hanging a mirror or planning storage. If she can't reach the hanging rod in the closet, she is not going to put away her clothes. Make it easier for her by installing a rod within her reach.

TOP
Boldly painted drawer fronts turn this ordinary nightstand into a work of art. Colorful gingham bedding looks fresh and inviting.

RIGHT
A shared nightstand is fine between two twin beds. Pretty beading on the lampshade adds a fun, feminine touch.

Furnishings

Furnishings that help to organize the room will keep your stress level down while adding to the overall livability of the space and comfort of your child. Multifunctional furniture may address all of your child's lifestyle needs in one room. The key is to know specifically what those needs are. Every child is different. Some kids don't insist on their own computer; they're fine using the one in the family room. Even a desk can be optional if your kids do their homework at the kitchen table (and you like it that way). Eliminating some of these items leaves space for a dressing table, perhaps, or an armoire for a TV or extra clothing storage. So, just as you would analyze your own needs when furnishing other rooms in the house, do the same with your child's room before furnishing it. Unless you're really adamant about having matching pieces, avoid furniture suites. Individual pieces look less fussy and allow you buy what you need. Also, refer back to

checklist

More clothes and toys, books, homework papers, awards, collections, and hobbies will require more organization and storage for your primary-school-age child. Here's a checklist of basic furniture necessities.

✓ Bed
✓ One or more freestanding or built-in chests of drawers
✓ A freestanding desk or a built-in desk or desk shelf (30 inches high)
✓ Shelving
✓ Nightstand
✓ Lighting
✓ Flooring

Chapter 3, "Great Furniture," which begins on page 50, for insights about furniture quality and how to look for it when you're shopping.

The Bed. Remember, at this age your child's universe begins to broaden, and he will start to develop friendships. That means he may soon want occasional sleepovers with friends. It's not a bad idea to plan for sleepovers when you're deciding on what type of bed to buy. Bunk beds are one way to go. Other options include a bed with a trundle or a double bed. If there's enough space in the room for a love seat or chair that opens into a sleeper, either one offers another solution. If all you can manage is a simple twin-size bed, relax: kids are adaptable. They love an excuse for camping out on the floor either in a sleeping bag or with just an extra blanket and pillow for the night.

Storage. Because most parents only want to purchase furniture once, items that will adequately serve your child's needs through the teen, and possibly college years, are the most practical. Avoid styles that are too cute or juvenile. A little girl who likes white painted furniture adorned with painted ribbons and bows will hate it when she's a "sophisticated" 15-year-old. It's a better idea to leave the sweet stuff for the accessories.

To suitably store clothes for your growing child, choose a double- or triple-width dresser. The latter is usually a combination of drawers and behind-door storage. Style doesn't matter: it's better to buy something that will fit in the space that you have.

Don't forget to take measurements of the room and compare them to the specifications for each piece of furniture that you plan to buy. Never make assumptions about size. Measure everything because so-called standard sizes can vary from one manufacturer to the next. If you can, purchase a chest (generally, just a taller set of drawers), with deep drawers that can hold bulkier items, such as off-season clothing, heavy sweatshirts and sweatpants, jeans, or an extra blanket.

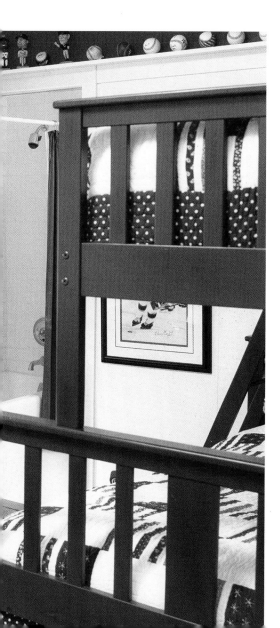

OPPOSITE TOP
A futuristic-looking chair in bold primary colors works perfectly in this boy's room.

LEFT
A built-in desk with cabinetry and drawers provides computer space and an additional work area. Task lighting is mounted to the underside of the bookshelves.

RIGHT
Ambient lighting is not sufficient for young students. A desk surface should include good, glare-free task lighting.

An armoire is a versatile item that can be outfitted to hold a TV, stereo equipment, and a computer with all of its related accoutrements. Or, you can equip the piece with shelves and a hanging bar for clothes storage. As an investment, an armoire is worth its cost many times over because, with modest retrofitting, you can use it in multiple ways in almost any room in the house.

A night table next to the bed can hold a lamp and an alarm clock. One table on each side isn't necessary if you don't have the space, but plan for at least one. You can also use a small chest, a covered table, or even a storage cube.

Although a desk is optional, it does provide a place for a computer and for organizing schoolwork, books, and some hobby materials. School-age children accumulate tons of paperwork, and you may want to save some of it. Consider an inexpensive two-drawer office file cabinet to store these keepsakes. You can spray-paint it to match the room. For important memos and party invitations, install a bulletin board, which can also display favorite photos and artwork.

Don't forget to include some kind of shelving to hold favorite collections, trophies, books, or other items you'll want to display. Always make sure that shelves are well anchored and cannot topple over. If the unit is free-standing, put heavier items on the bottom shelves and bolt the unit to the wall.

Lighting. Proper lighting becomes more important, especially ambient and task lighting. It's often said that a good lighting scheme is seldom noticed while bad or insufficient lighting is recognized instantly. Aside from brightening the room and eliminating eyestrain, the right lighting complements your decorating efforts. It makes colors ring true, and makes people feel better.

Besides general (ambient) lighting, such as a ceiling-mounted fixture or recessed ceiling canisters, plan to keep a light next to the bed. When reading in bed, your child will be lower to the mattress than an adult. Adjustable lamps with articulated arms are wise choices, since they can be positioned to meet a child's changing needs as he grows.

Include sufficient task lighting at the desk. Ideally, the bottom of the lampshade should stand about 15 inches above the work surface. The shade itself should measure 16 inches wide at the bottom, 14 inches wide at the top, and have a depth of 10 to 12 inches. Place the lamp on the right side of the work surface if your child is left-handed or to the left if she is right-handed. Collections and awards displayed on shelves can be illuminated, too. If you will be installing built-in furniture, such as a wall system, it can be equipped with light. Or consider installing recessed fixtures or strip lights that can be focused on a particular object or area. See "Lamps and Other Lighting Fixtures," on page 68 of Chapter 3 for more advice.

OPPOSITE
Mounted over the bed, this scoreboard clock becomes a witty focal point for the room. A sizable framed art piece or poster would work equally well.

RIGHT
Look for storage solutions that offer form as well as function. This inexpensive CD rack was painted to complement the decor.

Flooring. To create a cohesive scheme, choose a flooring material that will complement the room's decor. Either natural wood or a laminate look-alike work well with country, traditional, or period furnishings. An area rug, anchored with a nonskid mat, can enhance the design and add comfort without compromising safety. A hooked, braided, or rag rug has particular appeal in a country setting. If you choose a busy print for the wallpaper or curtains, pull out a solid accent color from the pattern and select a matching solid-color or mini-print rug. If other surfaces are plain, you may want to liven up the room with a bold-patterned area rug or a colorful painted floorcloth.

Wall-to-wall carpeting complements contemporary designs, but it is appropriate for any type of decor. To reinforce a modern theme, pick a geometric pattern or a solid color. There are also styles to coordinate with traditional furnishings. An Oriental or floral print rug is a good choice for coordinating with traditional rooms. For more information on various options for flooring, see page 90 in Chapter 4.

Accessories. A doll collection, trophies, snow globes, wind-up toys, action figures, ceramics, miniatures, or any objects of fascination are details that bring something of your child's personality into the room. This is a great time to start a collection with your child. What to collect? It can be funny hats, unusual flea-market finds, ceramic figurines, special posters or prints—anything that captures his or her imagination. Create a display on walls and shelves. Let your child create his own art and frame it. If wall space is at a premium, hang art on the closet door or install shelves above the window frames.

OPPOSITE
Your child's idea of what looks appealing probably doesn't match yours. If baseball is his passion, give it space.

RIGHT
This painted sea motif is augmented with actual fishing accessories.

BELOW RIGHT
Keepsakes, knick-knacks, autographs, and baseball cards, these are the treasures of childhood. Create a display of favorite things.

smart tip

SELF-ESTEEM BOOSTER

Children love to know how proud you are of their achievements, no matter how minor. Setting aside a portion of a wall to showcase school papers, whether they're tests, book reports, or artwork, is a great way to emphasize the importance of your child's successes. You can do this simply with a large corkboard or a magnet board. Another way is to set up mini-clotheslines across the wall with colorful plastic clothespins for displaying work. You can offset the area with a sign that reads, "Johnny's Masterpieces," or something to that effect. You can also frame and display his artwork elsewhere in the room.

decorating

Regardless of what kind of wallpaper you think might look nice, from this point on, your child will want to add her opinion to the discussion. Don't worry too much about formal decorating; your child will add personality to the space in her own way. Posters, activity schedules, and her framed artwork will take the place of the baby quilt and nursery-age pictures and accessories that you chose for her the last time around. To keep thumbtack and tape marks to a minimum, look for lightweight acrylic frames to display her best paintings and drawings. This type of frame will make it easy to change the artwork and update the collection with new ones whenever your child desires.

As soon as your child begins sports, dance, music, or some other hobby or activity, she will bring home trophies, ribbons, and certificates to display. Shelves are perfect for storage or collectibles, but also for showing off your child's accomplishments. A large corkboard is great for stickers, memos, school-achievement certificates, and photos of friends. If you want to make it special, cover the cork surface with leftover wallpaper. To eliminate the need for tacks and pushpins, wrap the board with cotton batting; then cover it with fabric. Use ribbon or fabric tape to create a diamond-trellis pattern. Then you can simply tuck pictures or cards inside the ribbon. You can upholster an area on a wall or a folding screen this way to create a larger display as well. See the next page for easy step-by-step instructions.

OPPOSITE
A custom closet and drawers built into the wall frees floor space and eliminates the need for bulky dressers.

ABOVE
Don't rush to fill every space with accessories. Soon enough, trophies, awards, and artwork from school will need a showcase.

safety counts

Even though your school-age youngster has progressed beyond the baby stage, you should take these measures to ensure that his room is safe.

- Install a smoke alarm above the door.
- Put away toys and keep the floor clear at night so that your child won't trip if he gets up to use the bathroom.
- Install a cool-to-the-touch night-light.
- Don't run electrical cords under rugs. Keep them tucked away behind furniture to prevent tripping
- Never use any electrical device with a torn or frayed cord.
- Use nonskid mats under area rugs. Make sure carpeting is securely tacked down.
- Attach bookcases and shelves securely to walls. Store heavy items on bottom shelves.
- Don't use glass-topped furniture.
- Make sure the bedroom door cannot be locked.

making an upholstered collectibles board

You can create a pretty spot to display anything from postcards to report cards in just a few easy steps. You don't need special skills or tools, and all it takes is a few minutes to a few hours (depending on the size of the surface you plan to cover). All that's important is that you take accurate measurements. This is a fun activity to enjoy with your child.

Older children may even want to do this project on their own. You can adapt this idea to fit the surface of a folding screen, a wall, or a closet door. Use corkboard or foam board, which should be available at an art-supply store. You'll need a measuring tape, scissors, and a staple gun. Fabric that's been leftover from another

project, such as curtains, a dust ruffle, throw pillows, or cushions, will do fine. However, you can also use a flat bed sheet or scraps from the fabric store. If you use a multicolor print, select the color of the ribbon or fabric tape from one of the hues in the fabric. If the fabric is a solid, choose a contrasting color or, if you are using ribbon, a print.

Start by measuring the board. You'll need a piece of cotton batting and a piece of fabric that is large enough to cover the front of the board plus a few extra inches to wrap around all four sides. Attach the cotton batting to the back of the board with staples. Miter the corners for a neat, custom finish. Do the same with the fabric. Then cut enough strips of ribbon or fabric tape to create your pattern. To make the diamond-lattice pattern featured here, make diagonal rows with the strips of ribbon. Work first from left to right; then from right to left. Attach the strips with upholstery tacks or sew-on buttons. Tuck pictures, cards, and other mementos underneath the ribbon strips.

YOU WILL NEED

- Measuring tape
- Scissors
- Corkboard (or similar surface)
- Cotton batting
- Fabric
- Coordinated ribbon or fabric tape
- Upholstery tacks or buttons
- Staple gun

ABOVE
A pair of companion paintings over the dresser pulls together the warm colors used throughout this room and provides a pretty focal point. Furnishings with clean lines and sprightly printed fabrics give the room a fresh, relaxed appeal.

Finishing Touches

By now, you have a good idea of your child's interests, hobbies, and preferences. This should help you to find a theme that can pull the entire room together. Sometimes something as simple as a wallpaper border is all you need. Fortunately, many manufacturers make themed borders that illustrate motifs popular with this age group. These include everything from dancing to music to sports, and they are easy to put up or take down.

Another method for carrying through a theme is to create a fabric-covered cornice for the window treatment. You can coordinate the cornice with the border or wallpaper. Although this is is a semipermanent window treatment, the cornice's covering can be altered or changed. At first, you can install the cornice on its own or over a fabric rollershade for a simple and understated look. When it is time to update the room, you can change the shade for another style or install shutters or curtains without needing to replace the cornice fabric.

design workbook

GIRLS JUST WANNA HAVE FUN

girl power

A delicately scrolled headboard and footboard set the tone for a girl's room that revels in its own femininity. Note the fringed lampshade and flower-accented chandelier adorned with pink crystals.

bejeweled

Floppy hats and fancy beads, top left, dress up this vintage dressing table. (See also below left.)

star struck

A kid-sized clothing rack, far left, keeps tutus and frilly dresses ready for an impromptu performance.

holding pattern

Pretty decorative hooks hold scarves and bags to accessorize the room's dress-up theme, left.

design workbook

DOWN BY THE SEA

high tide

This spectacular room was designed to look like a luxurious castaway's lair. The custom bed is finished to resemble driftwood, neutral carpet stands in for sand, and window treatments are arranged to look like fishing nets. A sea and sky mural completes the beachy scene.

catch my drift

All the wood in the room, including the dresser and "beach shack," top left, has a driftwood finish.

private cabana

The shack, top left, houses a desktop for schoolwork and crafts. Barrels fitted with striped fabric, left, provide seating.

private island

A reading loft with its own ladder, far left, adjoins the desk area. Pillows are piled below for playing on the floor with friends.

8

stylish
teen havens

**DO IT THEIR WAY   GETTING STARTED   A ROOM PLAN
FINISHING TOUCHES   DESIGN WORKBOOK**

I t's only a matter of time until your adolescent lets you know that he's outgrown his kiddy room. At this stage, you are not so much decorating a room for him as you are doing it with him. In fact, renovating the room may be entirely his idea. Most likely, he will have definite changes he wants to make, and you'll have to accommodate his preferences, as well as his lifestyle needs, which are increasingly more grown-up. Toys and other embarrassing reminders of young childhood are out. Teenagers require more storage for clothing, their expanding music collection, their computer apparatus, and assorted electronic equipment; they need a personal grooming spot and a place to do an increasing amount of homework. On top of all this, they want an environment that they can consider private, secure, and totally their own.

**LEFT
Many teens embrace bold colors and quirky accessories. Let the room reflect what is most special to them.**

Decorating a room for an older child can be challenging, but it can be accomplished without too much stress—especially if you remain open-minded and don't try to impose all of your ideas on the project. Just as she has developed her own personal style in clothing, books, music, and the people she befriends, she is finding her way in the decorating world, with ideas that may be unlike your own. There will be mistakes, but remember when she took her first wobbly steps? You didn't criticize her if she stumbled then, so don't do it now.

Of course, as a parent, you can set the ground rules, disallowing anything you find to be really outrageous, in questionable taste, or simply beyond your means. However, you may be pleasantly surprised and even proud of your teenager's creativity in the end.

do it their way

Color is one area that can be a source of contention between parents and children—particularly when a teenager chooses an unconventional or particularly jarring color scheme. If it's something that you think is too unusual or strong for the walls, suggest a compromise, such as bringing in touches of the color with linens, window treatments, or accessories.

At this age, boys as well as girls want a room that reflects their individuality and independence. Boys may or may not be as interested in the style of the curtains as girls, but they know what they don't like. Even if your teenage son says he doesn't care about the wallpaper pattern, don't assume he's going to be happy with something you might think is appropriate. If he doesn't want to get very involved in directly selecting a color scheme or textiles,

ABOVE
Whether parents approve or not, a video game nook has become a central feature of many teenagers' bedrooms.

OPPOSITE
A full-size bed and extra chair allow plenty of space for teens and their guests to comfortably hang out.

bring home samples of fabrics, wallpaper, and paint chips and ask him to eliminate anything he really doesn't like. That way you can discard the absolute no-no's before you make the final selection on your own.

Aside from decorating issues, teenage boys and girls share things in common in terms of room requirements. First, they want privacy. Unlike the days when they sat and watched TV in the family room or did their homework at the kitchen table while you prepared dinner, they spend most of their time in their rooms. There's no need to be alarmed. Your teenager isn't withdrawing, just growing up. Besides, kids of this age need a place to study or talk with friends without the distractions of the rest of household. Today, that often means designing a sociable space with an efficient workstation that is equipped with a computer and a printer, a comfortable and ergonomic chair, and sufficient storage for CDs and other supplies.

Many teens either have cell phones or their own phone line, which isn't a bad idea considering the time they could be spending tying up the house phone. An extra line only costs a few dollars a month, and it can be used for Internet access, as well, if you permit it. This is an added bonus, because instant messaging won't eat up valuable cell phone minutes.

Don't forget to make room for visiting friends. When kids of this age get together, they want to talk where you can't listen. Again, this is normal. Essentially, it's kids gradually separating themselves from their parents. Giving them the space, physically and psychologically, helps them to move toward adulthood. Besides, have you ever listened to teenage "conversation"?

getting started

Think of your teenager's bedroom as the precursor to her college dorm room. It's her sleeping space, her study and work niche, her place to entertain, and her private domain where she can talk about boys, hang crazy posters on the wall, and just be alone with her thoughts and dreams if she wants. What's more, if it's comfortable, she'll spend a lot of time there rather than in someone else's home.

By all means, encourage your teenager to become involved with the decorating and renovation process. Ask him to stop by the paint store and pick up color chips. Tell him to select a couple of rolls of wallpaper he likes that you can look over together. Follow these steps to get your teenager to take more interest in and responsibility for the project.

OPPOSITE
Adolescence is a time of great growth and change. Having a home base that envelops your teen in comfort and surrounds her with her favorite colors, textures, and mementos that make her smile is especially meaningful during this stage.

furnishings checklist

In the teen years, storage needs increase along with the need for extra seating pieces for studying and entertaining friends. Consider the following items:

- ✓ Bed
- ✓ Double- or Triple-Width Dresser
- ✓ Tall Chest of Drawers or Armoire
- ✓ Desk and Adjustable Desk Chair
- ✓ Shelving or Bookcases
- ✓ Extra Seating
- ✓ Nightstand or Bedside Table
- ✓ Lighting Fixtures
- ✓ Flooring

smart steps
chill teen digs

Step 1 WORK OUT A BUDGET TOGETHER
Tell her how much you can afford to spend, and then let her decide how to divvy up that amount on individual expenditures. If there's something she wants that your budget can't accommodate, perhaps she can contribute some of her savings or money from a part-time job. Or, instead of paying a contractor to paint the room, suggest to your teenager that if she does the work, the money saved can be spent on something that was off-limits before—the installation of special lighting, perhaps, or a high-speed Internet hookup.

Also, it's not hard to find inexpensive knockoffs of very trendy items. Very often, you can find a stylish look-alike of something he wants just by shopping around or by checking online.

Step 2 LET HER DO THE WINDOW-SHOPPING
Magazines, catalogs, the Internet, and even TV shows are good places to find ideas. Tell her to keep notes with the names of patterns, colors, and style numbers, as well as prices. Suggest that she tear out pictures from magazines or print out pertinent product information from her favorite design show's Web site. Hand her a pad of sticky-notes and ask her to tag catalog pages. You can go over these things with her when you're ready to shop. If there's a decorators' showhouse event in your area at the time (usually, around the holidays and in the spring), attend it together to see what designers are doing.

Step 3 BE THE PRACTICAL ONE
Determine the room's measurements, and take along the measuring tape when you go shopping. These are some of the details that he'll regard as tedious and will be happy to leave to you. Draw the line on renovations such as custom-painted murals on the walls, carpeting in an unusual color, or surround-sound speakers. These are not only expensive purchases, but will require replacement when your teenager leaves for college and you want to repurpose the room.

a room plan

If you've never evaluated your child's room in terms of size and shape, do it now so that you can maximize its potential. You'll be eliminating a lot of items that your teenager has outgrown, so you may be able to improve the room's existing floor plan and furniture placement. If you are purchasing new or additional furnishings, this step is essential. For more help, review "Evaluating the Space," on page 15, in Chapter 1.

After years of accumulating lots of stuff, this is a good time to decide what stays, what goes into storage, and what goes into the garbage. Host a yard sale for any toys she doesn't want to save. Use the earnings toward a purchase for the new room. Better yet, donate old toys that are in good condition to a local church, day-care center, or the children's ward of a hospital.

A good way to evaluate the architectural aspects of a room is to empty the space completely. That way you can see its bones and check out the condition of the walls, floor, windows, doors, and trim. After years of living, you may notice that some things need a little patching or more than a coat of fresh paint, especially in a boy's room. Even if all you have to do is install wallpaper and hang new curtains, you'll find that the job goes a lot

more easily in a room that isn't filled with furniture. When you're ready to put furniture back into the room, try a few sample arrangements on paper first. To help you do this, see the furniture templates in the Appendix.

Setting Aside A Place for Grooming

Personal appearance takes on new importance for girls and boys in the teen years. Providing a suitable spot someplace other than a main bathroom for grooming and storing toiletries will avoid conflict during busy times of the day.

If your teenager has her own bathroom, a spacious vanity or cabinet will contain her grooming products and also provide a place to primp. If not, think about ways to accommodate these needs in the bedroom. Certainly, a well-lit vanity table and mirror is one solution. Just make sure that there are adequate receptacles for small appliances, such as a hair dryer or a curling iron. A full-length mirror (freestanding or mounted to the back of a door) for checking overall appearance and a three-way dresser or vanity mirror to check hair helps. A space-saving lighted makeup mirror that can sit on a shelf or on top of a small, skirted table is another option. You can store cosmetics and small appliances in baskets underneath. Or keep toiletries neatly tucked into pretty hatboxes that can be left on display. Hang a shoe organizer on a hook or inside the closet. Use its deep pouches to handily store hair accessories, combs and brushes, and small cosmetics. Include a small wastebasket in the grooming area, too.

If there isn't enough room for a designated grooming area, adding a mirror over a desk can serve the same purpose, especially if the lighting can be adjusted for separate tasks. (See "Lamps and Other Lighting Fixtures," on page 68 in Chapter 3.) Reserve one of the desk drawers for grooming aids, and mount a hook to the inside wall under the desk in the leg area to hang a blow-dryer. Small storage boxes on top of the desk can hold paper clips, magnets, and other items.

Planning a Teen's Work Area

If you haven't already done so, you're probably going to have to set up a computer station in the room as well. If your son or daughter has been using the family computer until now, and that arrangement is still satisfactory with all parties, fine. If not, and you're ready to take the plunge, don't worry: it can be functional and comfortable without looking like tech central.

OPPOSITE
A lovely, well-lit spot for grooming in your teen's bedroom affords her the privacy she craves and cuts down on time spent in the family bathroom.

BELOW
Cubbies, drawers, and containers help organize the clutter that accumulates on the desktop, ensuring fewer distractions at homework time.

In addition to a computer, there is the related equipment. It's unwise to keep electronics on the floor because dust and dirt can damage these items, as can static from a rug or carpeting. So you'll need a desk or a flat surface with cubbies or shelves to house everything from a hard drive, printer, monitor, and possibly a scanner to CDs, headphones, and paper. It should be large enough to accommodate a legal-size notepad, as well as a keyboard and monitor. A rollout tray for the keyboard is a practical option because it places the keyboard at a comfortable level while freeing up room on the desktop. It's important to have a place where papers and items of different sizes can be stored out of sight. Otherwise, you're inviting a mess.

An adjustable chair is essential; a 13-year-old boy will sit taller at 14, and again at 15, and 16, and 17. So make sure the chair is ergonomically sound and offers ample comfort and support for the back of a growing adolescent. And don't overlook proper lighting. Your teenager will need adequate indirect illumination of the work surface. Avoid aiming light directly at the monitor, which will cause glare, or on the desktop, which will produce shadows.

In a room where space is tight, a laptop computer offers a solution. You can link it to a printer elsewhere in the house. Many laptop computers offer wireless Internet access. Otherwise, your teenager can browse the Web through a modem.

You'll also be happy to know that this equipment is increasingly available in versions that take up less space and will fit on a compact surface. For example, there are now flat-panel monitors and scaled-down hard drives that may cost more, but don't require a massive computer station to house them.

If your teenager doesn't want to look at electronic contraptions when they're not in use, no problem. You can house a computer and all of its accoutrements behind closed doors in either a custom-made or manufactured computer cabinet or armoire. Some of these cabinets come with a drop-down desktop. Just fold it back and close the doors for the look of an orderly room in an instant—every mother's dream.

If two teenagers share a room, you can design a double-length work center with space at each end for a computer, a monitor, and under-desk drawer storage, plus shelving. Both can share the printer and the scanner, if there is one.

Or, you can design a work surface that doesn't have to be placed up against the wall. That way, two siblings can sit on either side of the desk. The computer setup can consist of one computer, one printer, two monitors, and two keyboards. Teens can then network for files and games. In a shared work center, each area should also have its own task light and comfortable desk chair as well. Chairs on wheels can easily be rearranged for extra seating when their friends visit.

ABOVE

Cork and metal magnet boards are a great way to display favorite photos and keepsakes. A roomy bookshelf that accommodates storage boxes will go a long way toward keeping the bedroom clean and neat.

OPPOSITE

This well-designed computer station has plenty of storage and a good source of task lighting. The comfortable chair can be adjusted for height as your teen grows.

Furnishings

Sometimes teenagers want to make a complete change in the design or decor of their rooms. Adult furniture is on their list, and if you can afford it, you may go along with this request. But think before you leap into that purchase. In just a few years when he goes off to college, do you plan to keep the room for his visits home or convert it for another purpose? Will you let him take the furniture when he's ready to move out on his own? How much longer do you plan to actually remain in the house? Can you take the furniture with you if you go?

Specific furniture styles may mean more to your teenager as she begins to realize her own defined sense of style. But sometimes you can re-fashion older furniture by adding a new finish or treating it with one of the decorative paint finishes that are so popular. One new or refurbished piece of furniture can make a big change in the look of the room.

It's not difficult to create a simplified version of the upholstered bed on page 152. Here's how:

Trace the shape of your headboard onto kraft paper. Cut it out and use it as a template to cut a piece of 2-inch foam. Place the foam against the headboard. Cover both with a layer of fiber-fill batting and your fabric on top (add 3 inches, on all sides, to the dimensions of both). Wrap the batting and the fabric around to the back of the headboard and staple.

The Bed. At best, a mattress will continue to provide adequate support for about 12 years, but some health experts believe it should be replaced much sooner than that. Certainly, if it's worn, lumpy, or fails to provide a comfortable night's sleep, it should go. See the section called "Beds and Mattresses," which is on page 52 in Chapter 3, for advice about shopping for a quality mattress and box spring.

TOP LEFT

If your teen prefers you to take charge of the decorating scheme for his room, look for ways to incorporate his interests while maintaining the right balance of colors, textures, and fabrics.

LEFT

A new look doesn't always require new furniture. A coat of paint can turn an old piece into something bold and jazzy.

OPPOSITE

Many teenagers are budding artists just looking for an outlet. If your teen is talented, let him design and paint a mural, border, or faux finish on the walls and door of his room.

Your teenager and her friends will flop all over the bed. Extra throw pillows and bolsters can make this "seating" arrangement more comfortable.

Other bedding options that appeal to younger tastes include futons and daybeds. A better-quality futon offers enough support for nightly use, but shop and choose carefully. A futon is a good option for extra seating, as it can be converted easily into an extra bed for friends who want to crash overnight. A daybed can double as seating, too, but it has the advantage of a standard twin-size mattress. Many come with a trundle that slides out from under the daybed. Others feature a pop-up mechanism that elevates the trundle mattress to the height of a bed mattress.

smart tip

ORGANIZING CHAOS

How can you keep a teenager's room looking tidy? Don't leave things out in full view. Anything you can't fit behind closed doors should go into baskets or attractive boxes that are inexpensive, colorful, and designed to house everything from tiny hair clips to school papers. Open shelves can be organized this way. Look for special containers and racks to hold photographs, CDs, tapes, or just junk. They come in a wide assortment of colors and look great.

BELOW
Clever rollout shelves in a bedroom closet provide loads of extra storage, one of the best defenses against your teen's messy housekeeping habits.

OPPOSITE
Allow your teen to please all her moods—especially her sense of humor—with the accessories she chooses for her room.

Storage. One of the best things you can do is invest in a closet system. If it's in the budget, let an expert design and build it for your teenager's exact needs. Otherwise, a prefabricated system will do the job just fine. It's also wise to provide as many chests as possible in the room. A double- or triple-width dresser with a large mirror is good for starters. If there's room, include a tall chest of drawers. It's important to have adequate storage for bulky sweaters and sweatshirts, so look for units that have drawers that are deep enough to accommodate them without crushing them.

For extra blankets and pillows or out-of-season clothing, don't give up precious space in the closet. A storage trunk or armoire can easily house these items, as well as serve multipurpose needs. Add a rod to an armoire and you've created a wardrobe; install shelves and use the piece to hold a TV, DVD player, or other electronics. A trunk can double as a low table, too. So can a storage ottoman. You can recycle both of these pieces in other rooms of the house later.

Additional storage pieces can include a lingerie chest, a vanity, and nightstands. But don't forget to make use of every inch of space. The toys that once cluttered the shelves can now hold a sound system, CDs and tapes, speakers, books, collections, and even clothing. Use the space under the bed with drawers on castors that slide in and out easily. Install a closet system.

In addition to the custom-built computer center mentioned earlier, you have the option of a freestanding desk. If there is a computer and related equipment, look for a desk that is designed specifically for these items. You can find them in various sizes, configurations, and price ranges to suit almost any room. If you're handy with a screwdriver, a ready-to-assemble (RTA) unit is affordable for all budgets.

Some desks come with compartments that hide electronic gadgets for anyone who doesn't like the look of high-tech. A small filing cabinet is a must if the desk doesn't come with drawers. A rolling cabinet that can be pushed underneath the desktop is convenient, but be sure to check the clearance first.

Seating. In addition to a desk chair, additional seating is a consideration if there's room to accommodate it. A sturdy upholstered chair, love seat, or chaise lounge, accompanied by a floor lamp, is good for reading or studying. Beanbag or butterfly chairs offer appealing, young style.

Lighting. Good general and task lighting are essential ingredients in the room's design. Add accent lighting to illuminate framed prints, a collection on a shelf, or sports awards. A ceiling fixture or recessed canister lights provide efficient general illumination. Wall sconces and illuminated cove lighting are just two indirect solutions that are highly effective in a bedroom. In a large bedroom, consider spacing recessed fixtures about 8 feet apart for even lighting. An adjustable-arm or gooseneck desk lamp is fine at the desk for task lighting. For a dressing table or mirrored dresser, use wall sconces or table lamps at both ends to create even, shadow-free illumination for grooming.

An important thing to remember when choosing a lamp is that any flat, reflective surface can be the source of indirect glare, which causes eyestrain. Surfaces that are prone to indirect glare include shiny desktops, mirrors, glass-top surfaces, as well as TV screens and computer monitors. The solution is to aim the light source away from these surfaces. For example, place a reading lamp behind the reader's left shoulder.

Flooring. Don't overlook flooring and the role it plays in tying all of the room's surfaces together. Color and pattern choices depend largely on the rest of the room, but a light, neutral scheme offers the most versatility; flooring is a semipermanent element that shouldn't have to be replaced every time you change the color of the walls or the bedding.

In large rooms, an area rug over wood or resilient flooring

material adds warmth and coziness. Wall-to-wall carpeting, especially in a light solid color, visually expands the size of the room. It also has another advantage over most other types of flooring—it muffles sound. If you're looking for a way to cut down on the noise, this could be the answer.

You can't count on teenagers to be cautious about spills and splatters on the floor, so it's always a good idea to shop for materials that can stand up to the abuse kids of all ages can cause. Wood, laminate, and resilient flooring are easy to maintain and clean. Carpeting requires vacuuming and immediate attention when something is spilled on it. For practicality's sake, it's smart to buy a carpet with built-in stain resistance.

OPPOSITE
Providing frames for posters rather than taping or tacking them to the wall protects the walls and gives the room a more finished, refined look.

ABOVE
A vinyl floor offers the look of tile, but provides a softer impact underfoot. It is durable and easy to keep clean.

ABOVE RIGHT
With resilient flooring or carpet tiles, customizing a floor pattern to complement the room is easy and affordable.

RIGHT
Although spills may still occur, teens are not as rough on floors as younger children, so a hardwood floor can be a viable choice. Another option is a laminate wood floor.

finishing touches

Your teen's room should really be her project. The styles, colors, patterns, and accessories she chooses will reflect her point of view. However, you can still offer your guidance. Most teens seem to prefer informal furnishings punctuated by casual fabrics such as denim, velour, or cotton prints. For color inspiration, take a look at teen fashion. If their clothing has a retro-Seventies look, home fashions aimed at this market will reflect it in terms of color and motif. You'll find accessories from duvet covers to lampshades and picture frames available in a range of price points.

Your teenager's taste and sense of self may be different at age 17 than it is at age 13, so you'll have to find a way to keep fads and trends limited to items that can be changed without much fuss. Stick to items you can pick up inexpensively at a discount or chain store for adding a trendy look, and keep the major elements of the room simple.

teen room safety

Safety is important at all ages. Go over this list with your teenager, who is old enough to assume more responsibility for her own safety.

- Install a smoke alarm above the door.
- Keep books and clothing off the floor to avoid creating a tripping hazard, especially during the night.
- Don't run electrical cords under rugs. Keep them tucked away behind furniture. Never use a frayed or damaged cord. Don't overload plugs and extension cords.
- Install nonskid mats under area rugs. Make sure carpeting is securely tacked down.

LEFT
The architectural features of a room can often suggest unique opportunities for creating a dramatic focal point.

RIGHT
As a young person becomes more sophisticated in his taste, bedding, accessories, and artwork can be changed to reflect his expanding sensibilities.

design workbook

MARKET VALUE

just the thing

Some furniture retailers offer storage pieces designed for teens that can be customized to suit your child's room.

sliding storage

Underbed storage designed to look like vintage office cabinets, top left, is a fun, funky way to keep large items tucked away.

locker up

Popular "gym locker" storage bins, magazine files, drawers, and cabinets in varying sizes can contain anything from clothes to keep-sakes to sports equipment.

test your metal

Metal magnet boards, left, are the newest alter-native to cork boards. Look for magnetic tape that attaches photos and papers with-out the need for bulky magnets.

design workbook
MODERN ART INSPIRATION

mondrian style

In a tribute to this modern master's works, a teen artist's bedroom walls are painted in rectangles of primary colors separated by thin black lines.

warhol style

Photos taken with a variety of colored filters and then enlarged to poster size echo the unforgettable Marilyn Monroe montages made famous by artist Andy Warhol.

pollack style

The innovative Jackson Pollack might have appreciated the sheets used here, which call to mind his canvases of paint splatters and drips.

photo montage

Reflecting the aesthetic of modern photography, a unique mosaic arrangement of a street scene, left and top left, takes center stage over the bed.

9

special needs

When children are faced with physical challenges or medical conditions, their home should be a source of comfort rather than frustration. Depending on the circumstances, some environmental conditions can even exacerbate an illness. When that happens, a few thoughtful adaptations can make a child's room comfortable without sacrificing any of the fun stuff that makes it his own special place. By eliminating the obstacles that make him dependent upon others, you can help your special-needs child develop a can-do attitude that will carry him successfully through life. Gearing a room for use by any child is essentially creating an adapted environment. It only takes common sense—lowering storage, adjusting mirrors to an appropriate height, and keeping electrical cords and other objects out of harm's way.

LEFT
Daily vacuuming and keeping fabrics to a minimum can help to alleviate symptoms in an allergic child.

It's common for parents to look for furniture that's easy and comfortable for their children to use. Beds and chairs should be easy to access, shelves should be within reach, and handles, knobs, and pulls must be the right size and shape for small hands to grab. All of these efforts are intended to make kids independent, capable, and safe. Children are remarkably resourceful when it comes to getting what they want and need; a special-needs child just needs a bit of help to accomplish these goals.

levels of ability

When planning your room design, first determine what areas require your special consideration. Analyze your child in terms of the following:

■ **Fine motor skills** affect the ability to flip light switches, turn doorknobs, manage tasks on a smaller work surface, operate stereo and TV controls, and manipulate a computer keyboard.

■ **Upper body strength** is necessary to open doors, pull drawers, and carry heavier toys and other objects.

■ **Extent of reach** determines the ability to retrieve objects and control lighting and other electronics.

■ **Stamina** affects the ability to handle a wheelchair, climb stairs, open a heavy door, lift one's self in and out of bed, and cross the room in some cases.

■ **Gross motor-skill level** determines the ability to maneuver a wheelchair or walker precisely and negotiate the floor plan of the room.

In addition to physical limitations, a sensory deprivation such as visual impairment, blindness, and hearing loss will require some room adaptations. Allergic or asthmatic children can also benefit from rooms that are tailored to their specific needs for a meticulously dust- and allergen-free environment.

Your child's needs and the adaptations they require may be highly specific to her. But there are general steps you can take that can improve the livability of your child's room. Some adaptations are simply practical and can be achieved with ordinary materials; others may require specific products. Consult the Resource Guide, page 208, which may be helpful if you need to locate a special device. And don't forget to ask for your child's cooperation when you're planning the room's design. Ask her to point out things that may be helpful or to demonstrate how much turnaround space is necessary for her wheelchair. Ask what you can do to make moving around and using the furniture easier.

thoughtful flooring

For ease of exit and entry, make sure that any transition from a hard surface to carpeting is made more gradual with the use of metal threshold strips. Carpeting or matting should measure no more than one-half inch thick. Because wheelchairs and walkers can take a toll on the baseboards and make marks on painted surfaces, consider running the carpeting 4 or 5 inches up the wall.

The Bedroom Door

The bedroom door primarily provides access when it's open and privacy when it's closed. But the door can become a problem when the knob can't be turned, or when a wheelchair or a walker can't fit through the doorway. This can compromise your child's freedom to move in and out of his own room without help.

To make a door opening wheelchair- and walker-accessible, and to keep both equipment and little hands unscathed, the opening must be at least 32 inches wide. If it's not possible to widen the doorway, you can gain a few inches by reinstalling the door on offset or swing-clear hinges. There should also be a clearance of 18 inches of wall space next to the door handle. A tighter space will make it difficult if not impossible to grab and turn the handle or knob. If clearance is a problem, you can exchange the door for one that can be installed in the opposite direction. (Replace a door with a right-hand swing for one with a left-hand swing.) Replacing a standard door with a pocket door (one that slides into the wall) is another idea. An automatic door that works by remote control or on sensors can solve the problem, too, but this solution can be much more expensive than a standard door.

Door hardware can be another stumbling block. If gripping and turning knobs is a problem, replace them with lever or loop-type hardware. Add-on lever extensions can convert an ordinary knob. You can get one that installs permanently or one that travels with the child to provide access to doors throughout the house. Give any solution you use the closed-fist test—that is,

make sure you can open it easily with just one hand, closed into a fist. If your child has the use of only one arm, it may be helpful to reinstall the door so that the handle is easily accessible. You can apply many of these ideas to the closet door as well. The weight of the door can be an issue if your child has limited strength or stamina. Look for a lighter, hollow-core door to replace an existing solid-wood door.

Finally, getting the door open is not much use if the threshold presents yet another barrier. The best plan may be to eliminate it completely.

Layout and Furnishings

A wheelchair needs a 5-foot radius in which to turn around. Children using walkers need plenty of space to manipulate their equipment, too. When you're organizing the layout of your child's room, make good use of the available wall space. Your basic plan should be to keep the center of the room clear and to arrange all the furniture and activity stations against the walls. If the room is shared and contains two beds, make sure a 36-inch aisle exists between the beds and to any exit or activity area.

Because some special-needs children may find it difficult or impossible to play on the floor, install large desktop surfaces for games and hobbies. These surfaces can also work for homework projects and personal grooming tasks. Keep appropriate materials near their designated station for easy access. In the case of an older child, equip the tabletop with electrical outlets he can reach, such as a computer surge-protector strip, and be sure switches to control task lighting are also within reach.

A tabletop for an adult who uses a wheelchair should measure between 28 to 34 inches high; you'll have to measure to determine the height that is comfortable for your child. The depth of the table should be convenient to its user's ability to reach. Knee space should be 27 inches high, 30 inches wide, and 19 inches deep. A single large desktop, cantilevered from the wall and divided into different activity stations, is another good idea. It makes traveling between stations easy. Storage crates and shelves that house the materials to be used at each station can

LEFT
A visually impaired child might benefit from sharp color contrasts that outline and define different sections of the room.

OPPOSITE
A lighted closet with open storage makes finding clothing much easier and eliminates the need to manipulate dresser drawers.

also be used to differentiate each zone.

If a child who uses a walker must stand, or is more comfortable standing, to perform certain activities, consider an adjustable-height table that will accommodate her needs as she grows. An artist's drawing board might work for this application. Furniture designed to function as a freestanding kitchen or work cart is another option.

Bending down to pick up toys or materials that fall or roll off work surfaces is frequently impossible for a child with special needs. Attach hook-and-loop-type strips at the top and sides of the work surface and to each item that will be used in that station to eliminate this problem. This is also a good solution if the child uses items on a wheelchair tray. If the item is too large, or if you don't want to attach something quite as permanent as the hook-and-loop strips (on a computer keyboard, for example), try large C-clamps purchased from a hardware store. If the room is too small to accommodate a series of workstations, use a variety of wheelchair trays, customized for each of your child's activities.

Assuming Controls. Controls for lighting the room must be both reachable and workable. There are devices available at children's product stores that can replace an existing switchplate with one that is mounted lower on the wall.

If you lower light switches, raise the level of the electrical outlets at the same time. You can find adapters for electrical outlets that enhance their visibility; there are also products that make switching lights on and off easier for those with limited fine motor skills. One such product extends the outlet so that it protrudes an inch from the wall. The raised surface not only protects hands from potential shocks but creates a channel that helps guide the plug into the outlet. Lamps also can be adapted for kids with limited grasping ability by attaching spoke-style switches to existing ones. Look on the Internet or in related catalogs for many of these items.

If your child lacks the fine motor ability to manipulate any switch, consider a motion-sensor light as an ambient light source—it can be installed on a timer so that it shuts off at bedtime. Another option that has proven to be highly effective is a "clap-on, clap-off" lighting system. This can also be used to turn on a stereo, television, or computer.

There are many products that allow you to tailor electronic devices in a room for a person with specific limitations. The Education Development Center of the National Center to Improve Practice has compiled an extensive list of adaptive technology for computers to aid students who are visually impaired. (For additional information, see the Resource Guide on page 208.)

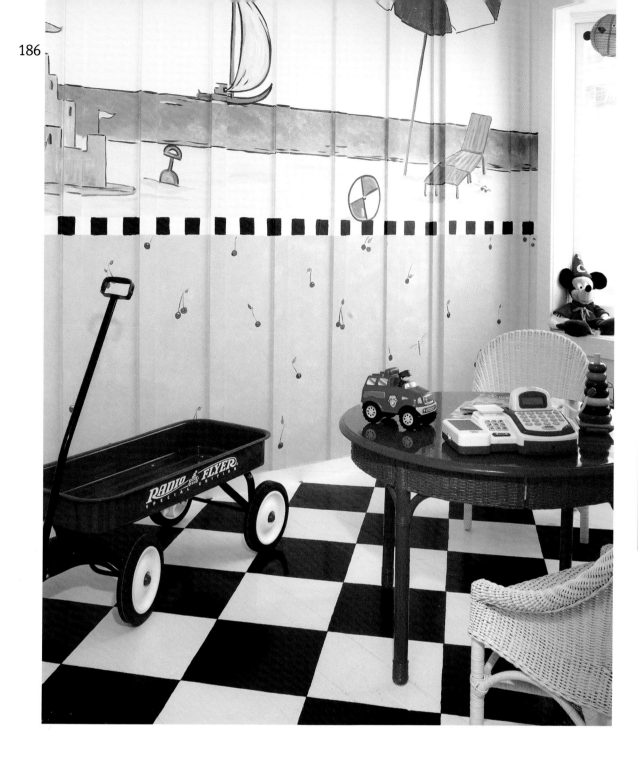

smart tip

LIGHTING AND COLORS FOR THE VISUALLY IMPAIRED

Visually impaired kids benefit from bright light but are hindered more than other kids by glare. Keep shiny surfaces that reflect light to a minimum. Position mirrors, the computer, and the TV so that they will not pick up glare from window light or artificial lighting sources. Bright contrasts—not necessarily bright colors—are most readily appreciated by kids with low vision. Use contrasting wall colors and patterned bedding, throw pillows, and window treatments for decoration. Reserve bright "warning" colors, such as orange, for marking changes in floor grade or "do not touch" spots.

Accessible Storage

Just as you would lower storage to accommodate little children, you can raise it to suit a child who cannot get down to floor level. Stacked crates are perfect for this purpose. Crates at the bottom of the stack can hold seldom-used items or the things you use to care for your child, while the upper crates can contain toys, games, books, and the usual array of kid stuff. Color coding the crates—especially useful for the visually impaired—will help children find just what want, whether it's the action figures in the red crate, the books in the yellow crate, and so on.

Look for dressers with drawers that open and close with a minimum of effort. Drawers on rollers are a perfect choice. Drawers constructed of lightweight material such as plastic, while usually too flimsy to stand up to "kid-force," can work well for a child with limited strength. If drawers are too difficult to handle, store clothing in cubbies attached to the wall at an accessible height. Wall-mounted cabinets usually found in the kitchen make great storage for kids who can't maneuver drawers but can manage cabinet doors.

Closet bars can be lowered. If the bar is permanently attached, install another one a bit lower on the wall. Automated devices that rotate clothing and make finding an item easier are available at home stores and through catalogs. Clothing can also be hung on a rack located outside the closet, as long as it remains neat. This is much more accessible for kids with wheelchairs and walkers. Shoes and accessories can be neatly hung on shaker pegs attached to the wall at the child's level.

allergy and asthma issues

The answer to keeping a bedroom free of allergens—agents such as dust mites, food particles, animal dander, plant and insect matter, mold and fungus, and bits of fabrics—is to create an environment inhospitable to the dust that carries them. The following Smart Steps will prepare the room initially; conscientious cleaning will keep it that way.

smart steps
eliminating allergens

Step 1 SEAL THE BED

Start by covering the bed's mattress and box spring in the airtight, washable plastic zipper covers made for this purpose. Pillows made of foam are preferable, but not the most comfortable choice. If your child needs a softer headrest, experiment with nonallergenic synthetic pillows. Avoid feather and down pillows completely. Like the mattress, cover the pillow with an airtight plastic case. Natural wool and cotton-fiber blankets are best. Wash all bedding weekly in very hot water to kill mites and remove skin particles. Some experts recommend changing to a clean pillowcase daily.

Step 2 GO EASY WITH FABRICS

Fabric accessories with their pleats, folds, and nap are notorious dust collectors. To combat this, keep window treatments spare and ban upholstered furnishings from the room. A simple roller blind, which is easier to dust than the slats of mini-blinds, will suffice. Find one that is printed to coordinate with the room. If you use a vinyl shade, you can stencil a design onto it. Fabric paint will work for your project if you use a blind made of canvas or another no-nap material.

Step 3 CHOOSE A HARD FLOOR SURFACE

Not only does carpeting collect dust, but the chemicals in its foam rubber padding can cause an allergic reaction. A hardwood floor is the best choice. When it's time to have the floor refinished, visit Grandma or go away for the weekend, leaving the windows open for several days if possible. Make sure the varnish has a low VOC (volatile organic compounds) rating. Have the floor professionally cleaned or rent a vacuum with a HEPA (high-efficiency particulate arrestance) filtration system to remove all traces of the sanding particles. Depending on the type of adhesive used, a vinyl floor is also suitable for this kind of installation—and it requires just a daily mopping. Low-pile area rugs that can be frequently washed will soften the floor for play.

Step 4 CLEAR THE AIR

Dry air is best for kids with allergies. Don't wait until the dog days of summer to use an air-conditioner; start running it as soon as allergy season begins in the early spring. To maintain an ideal humidity level (less than 50 percent), you may need a dehumidifier. Clean filters frequently and replace them when needed. If allergies are severe, a HEPA filtration unit may help.

Step 5 ELIMINATE UPHOLSTERY

Every time a plush seat is used, millions of tiny particles are propelled into the air your child breathes. Solid-wood or metal furnishings are easy to keep dust-free. Avoid heavy lacquers, paint or varnish, particleboard, or wood veneers that can emit fumes into the air.

Step 6 BANISH ANIMALS

Both the living kind and the plush variety are bad news for allergy sufferers. Even if the family pet is tolerable for the allergic child, keep him out of the bedroom. For a young child, choose one or two stuffed animals that are machine-washable. If a non-machine-washable favorite already exists, pop it into the freezer every so often to kill mites. Otherwise, wash the stuffed toys regularly along with the bedding. Even these precautions may not be enough to prevent attacks in some severely allergic children.

In general, the allergy sufferer's room should be easy to clean. Limit knickknacks. The fewer surfaces the room contains, the fewer places dust mites and mold can breed. Establish play and activity space elsewhere in the house, and limit furnishings to a bed and dresser. A child spends many hours in the room where she sleeps, so make it allergen-free.

smart tip
HEALTHY CLEAN

A number of "green" companies are now offering cleaning products that replace harsh or potentially harmful chemicals with natural products like vinegar and plant compounds. Not only are they healthier for you, they come in nonaerosol containers that are good for the environment.

ABOVE
Natural fabrics and materials are best for kids who are sensitive to their environment. Keep surfaces uncluttered so regular dusting is easy. Also, consider allergy-proof mattresses and pillow covers.

fine tuning

Whether it is breathing through a nebulizer for 15 minutes several times a day, receiving therapeutic massage, performing exercises, or enduring slow-drip intravenous medications, chances are children come to resent these necessary measures as intrusions on the business of being a kid. Make this time pass as quickly as possible by set-ting up an aquarium. If a treatment is rendered while your child lies in bed, a well-placed TV and game controls might provide a distraction. If viewing is not possible, look for books on tape.

For a child who is unable to help herself out of bed (also for one who receives treatment lying down in bed) invest in an overhead projector. Teaching-aids catalogs sell ready-made transparencies, or you can make your own. Adjust the projector so that the image appears on the ceiling. Affix the controls to the bed so that she can use them. An adjustable bed and wall-mounted TV may be another option.

design workbook
EASY-ACCESS DECORATING

no heavy lifting

Keeping the items that are used frequently in lightweight plastic storage bins and baskets makes possessions readily available and easy to retrieve. (See also below left.)

open to view

A system of cubbies, shelving, and racks keeps many other items in plain sight and eliminates drawers and doors that can present problems for some children. (See also below left.)

fewer fabrics

With a cozy blanket, some colorful toss pillows, and modest drapery, dust and allergens can be kept under control with regular vacuuming. (See also top left.)

smooth sailing

The choice of resilient flooring and a room plan that maximizes open space makes the room function better for a child with disabilities.

10
bathrooms
for kids

SENSIBLE AND BASIC   DESIGN WORKBOOK

Bathing is a key component of most people's daily routine, and children are no exception. Because learning good hygiene habits is an important part of growing up, a bathroom that is designed around a child's smaller size can be enormously helpful. You'll want a space that enables him to take charge of his morning and bedtime care with a minimum of effort. Special safety concerns should always take precedence over other design elements. If you share a bathroom with your child, take appropriate steps to accommodate his size and needs in addition to your own. Most newer homes contain a second bath, which is often designated for younger family members. What should be included there depends on the ages and number of children who will use it. If your child has the room all to himself, plan it for his growing and changing needs.

LEFT
This bath adjoining a child's room is playfully decorated with paint, wallcovering, and pretty cabinet pulls.

sensible and basic

There are many things you can do to make any bathroom practical, comfortable, and safe for family members of all ages. If you're planning to build or renovate a bath that will be used by you and your child, give careful consideration to the age-specific needs of the youngster.

Caring for Baby

The baby's bathroom should be a warm, draft-free environment. You should organize this space around your needs for bathing the baby. You'll want everything right at hand so you don't need to take your eyes off baby for even a moment. Remember: a child can drown in less than 2 inches of water in a portable baby tub or toilet, or even in a bucket filled with water.

Appropriate furnishings include a comfortable seating area where you can dry the baby or towel a toddler, a convenient place to house the baby bath, perhaps a changing table, and ample storage for the baby's toiletries and linens, diapers, bath toys, a hamper, and a diaper pail.

Consider your own comfort when positioning the baby bath. Counter height will probably be most comfortable, or you may consider a freestanding bathing unit. Install an anti-scald faucet, which contains a device that keeps water temperature constant. Because a child's skin is thinner and more tender than an adult's, it can be burned within 3 seconds after coming into contact with water that's more than 120 degrees Fahrenheit. Fixtures equipped with a pressure-balancing feature will maintain the same degree of heat even when cold-water flow is reduced (when you flush the toilet, for example). A single-lever faucet, as opposed to two separate valves, is much easier for a child to use when regulating water flow and temperature. You can preset some of these, as well.

A hand-held shower device that allows you to position the showerhead at a convenient level can be retrofitted onto a conventional showerhead or installed separately. Look for one that's been designed for children to handle.

Once you start to bathe the baby in the tub, you'll want to make it slip-resistant. A textured surface helps. You can easily add this with anti-slip decals and mats. Install soft covers over the faucet and spout to avoid bumping tender heads. Parents can

Anticipate the storage and lighting requirements of a teenage girl's grooming habits, for example. If more than one child will share the bath, consider their genders, and whether they will use the room at the same time. How many lavatories do they need? Assume that two is a reasonable number. The best designs for shared bathrooms include compartmentalized spaces—one for the toilet, one for bathing (with a separate shower, if space permits), and one for grooming. A double-bowl vanity is the most practical. At least try to set the toilet apart from the bathing area—even a half wall will help.

There are fixtures on the market that are tailored for a child's use, but you may not want to make the investment in something that will have to be replaced once your child grows or leaves home. As always, it's a matter of choice. If you want to make the room appealing to the younger set but your funds are limited, look into wallpaper patterns that have a juvenile theme and use lively, kid-friendly colors and accessories.

protect themselves by using a mat that extends over the side of the tub to cushion their arms while holding up and bathing the baby. Part of the mat also rests on the floor to pad adult knees.

It's a good idea to install easy-care wallcovering and flooring. From the first moment a baby learns to splash, dry surfaces become a memory. Classic selections include tiles, vinyl wallcovering with built-in mildewcide, solid-surfacing material, a fiberglass tub surround, and gloss or semigloss paint.

A one-piece toilet hugs closer to the wall and has an elongated bowl that makes toilet training a little easier. Because it sits lower than a two-piece model, this type is better scaled for a child yet still comfortable for an adult.

OPPOSITE
A bath adjacent to the nursery makes bath time more convenient and is handy for quick cleanups during diaper changes.

ABOVE
Where there is space, treat kids who share a room to double sinks in the bath. This way, two can prepare for school or bedtime simultaneously.

Helping Preschoolers

Toilet training and the beginning of self-grooming occur during the preschool stage, necessitating a few changes in the way your child will use the bathroom. Tubs and toys seem made for each other now. Gear toy storage to something your child can access himself, such as a plastic basket that can be kept inside a vanity cabinet or on the floor of the linen closet. You'll also need a place to keep a small step stool when it's not in use as a booster in front of the sink. If you're renovating or building a new bathroom for a child, consider installing a sink into a vanity or countertop that is built at a lower height.

Because the common rule of thumb is to install a mirror 8 inches above a standard-height vanity countertop (to avoid splatters), you may want to include a standing mirror or one that extends from the wall at a proper height to suit your child. To encourage neatness, a towel rack that is within a child's reach is another good idea. A low freestanding rack works well, too.

special soaps and shampoos, and other toiletries. Keep electrical appliances, such as hair dryers, steam rollers, or electric shavers, out of the room until your child is old enough to handle them responsibly and understands their potential hazards.

More about Shared Spaces. The crunch for bathroom time begins when kids start toilet training and continues through the school years when the whole family must get bathed, dressed, and out of the house at the same time. To cope with the increased demands, create private areas within the bathroom, such as the separate bathing, grooming, and compartmentalized toilet areas suggested earlier. Color-code towels and accessories so that every family member can clearly see what belongs to each person who uses the room.

Finally, move certain activities to other rooms. Dressing and grooming can be done in the bedroom, for example. Whether your home has one small bathroom that is shared by all or a separate bathroom for each member of the family, there are steps you can take to make the space more efficient.

Accommodating School-Age Kids

Socializing skills in school reinforce the needs for individual identity at home, including specific grooming styles as a child gets older. Storage niches once devoted to bathtub toys can be used for hair ornaments,

OPPOSITE
An extra-large sink gives you the option to bathe small children at a level that may be more comfortable for you than bending over the side of the tub. The large vanity provides extra storage space.

RIGHT
If the kids' bath is located away from the main linen closet, store extra towels on hooks. Roll washcloths, and keep them in a basket.

smart steps
build a better bath

Step 1 PLAN STORAGE

If you don't have a linen closet or large cabinet in the room, add shelving to hold extra towels, bars of soap, and other necessities. Small storage niches created between the wall studs make handy spots for shampoo and toiletries. Mount hooks or pegged racks to the wall or behind the door for hanging extra towels or robes. New medicine cabinets come with extra-deep shelves that are large enough to hold rolls of toilet paper or bulky appliances.

Step 2 CONSIDER A BETTER WAY TO USE SPACE

Cramped floor area? Replace the bathroom door with a pocket door, which can free up enough space for a separate shower stall or a double vanity.

Step 3 LIGHT IT PROPERLY

Besides general lighting, plan adequate task lighting at the sink and mirror for grooming. Avoid positioning lights above the mirror where they can create glare and shadows. Side lights are preferable.

Step 4 CLEAR THE AIR

Invest in a good exhaust fan to make the room's air quality healthier and surfaces less slick. A fan will also prevent water buildup and mildew, which can damage surfaces and fabrics.

RIGHT
Find more space by recessing shelving into the wall to accommodate linens and toiletries. A bold shower curtain, sink skirt, and rug contrast nicely with the more subdued wall and floor tiles.

OPPOSITE
Use rubber area-rug pads to prevent slipping. In a contemporary bath, clean lines and minimal clutter reflect the design aesthetic of the bedroom.

bathroom safety

Here's a list of things that you should have on hand at all times to make sure a bathroom intended for a child's use is safe and comfortable.

Tub and Shower Areas
- Safety glazing on glass doors
- Doors that are hinged to swing out into the room
- Grab bars at adult and child heights
- A shower seat

Toilets and Water Closets
- No lock on the water-closet door
- Locking toilet lid
- Tip-resistant training step stool
- Toilet-paper holder installed within the child's reach

Plumbing
- Water valves within easy reach
- Single-lever controls
- Anti-scald and pressure-balanced faucets
- Adjustable child-size hand shower

Electric
- Ground-fault circuit interrupters (GFCIs) on all outlets
- Covered receptacles

- Vapor-proof light fixtures installed out of the child's reach
- Low-voltage task lighting
- Night-light

Cabinet and Counter Surfaces
- Small doors that can be easily opened
- Childproof locks
- Locked medicine cabinet
- Maximum 8-inch-deep cabinets installed over the toilet
- Rounded corners and edges
- Seating for drying off and dressing

Flooring
- Nonslip surface
- Water-resistant surface
- Anchors for area rugs and mats

Windows and Doors
- Doors that swing into the room
- Door locks that can be opened from the outside
- Safety bars on all windows

design workbook

BATHING BEAUTIES

lime twist

Youthful colors enliven this room. Fresh green walls are accented with a striped shower curtain and drawer pulls in complementary hues.

recess time

A series of drawers set into the mosaic-tiled walls of this bath, top left, provides storage for towels and toiletries within a small space.

mod cons

A pullout hamper, with a paneled front that blends into the walls, left, keeps dirty towels, as well as dirty socks, off the floor and out of sight.

appendix TEMPLATES FOR KIDS' ROOMS

Window and Door Templates

Windows

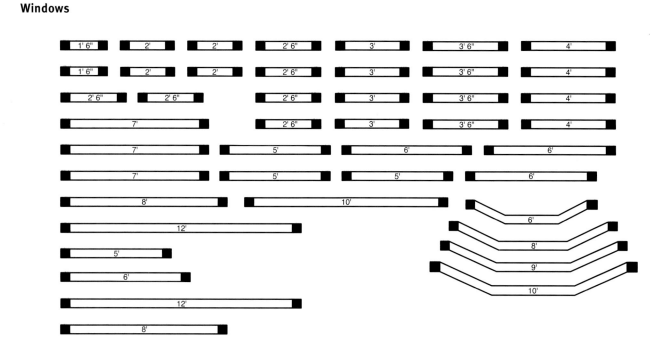

Doors

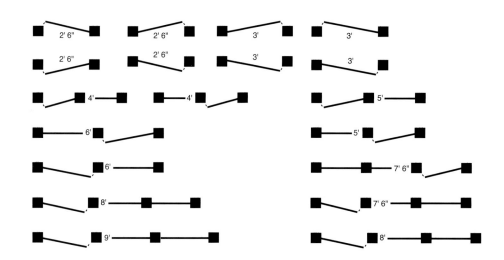

Furniture Templates

Beds

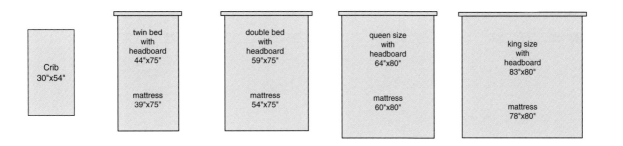

Crib 30"x54"	twin bed with headboard 44"x75" mattress 39"x75"	double bed with headboard 59"x75" mattress 54"x75"	queen size with headboard 64"x80" mattress 60"x80"	king size with headboard 83"x80" mattress 78"x80"

Case Goods

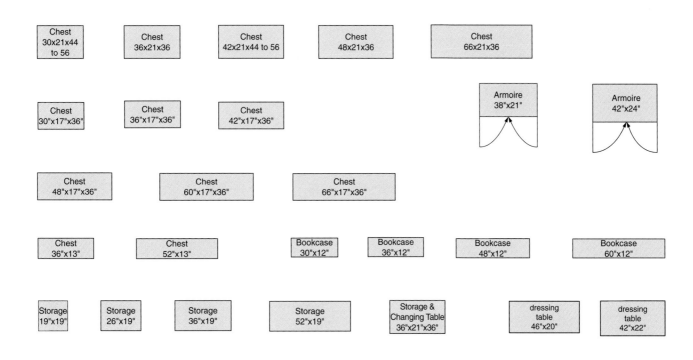

Chest 30x21x44 to 56	Chest 36x21x36	Chest 42x21x44 to 56	Chest 48x21x36	Chest 66x21x36
Chest 30"x17"x36"	Chest 36"x17"x36"	Chest 42"x17"x36"		Armoire 38"x21" / Armoire 42"x24"
Chest 48"x17"x36"	Chest 60"x17"x36"	Chest 66"x17"x36"		
Chest 36"x13"	Chest 52"x13"	Bookcase 30"x12"	Bookcase 36"x12"	Bookcase 48"x12" / Bookcase 60"x12"
Storage 19"x19" / Storage 26"x19"	Storage 36"x19"	Storage 52"x19"	Storage & Changing Table 36"x21"x36"	dressing table 46"x20" / dressing table 42"x22"

Furniture Templates

Built-In Cabinets

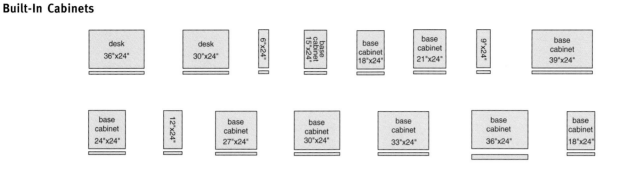

desk 36"x24"	desk 30"x24"	6"x24"	base cabinet 15"x24"	base cabinet 18"x24"	base cabinet 21"x24"	9"x24"	base cabinet 39"x24"

base cabinet 24"x24"	12"x24"	base cabinet 27"x24"	base cabinet 30"x24"	base cabinet 33"x24"	base cabinet 36"x24"	base cabinet 18"x24"

Tables and Desks

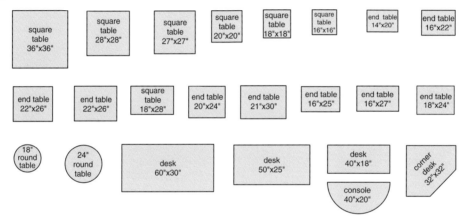

square table 36"x36" · square table 28"x28" · square table 27"x27" · square table 20"x20" · square table 18"x18" · square table 16"x16" · end table 14"x20" · end table 16"x22"

end table 22"x26" · end table 22"x26" · square table 18"x28" · end table 20"x24" · end table 21"x30" · end table 16"x25" · end table 16"x27" · end table 18"x24"

18" round table · 24" round table · desk 60"x30" · desk 50"x25" · desk 40"x18" · console 40"x20" · corner desk 32"x32"

Chairs and Ottomans

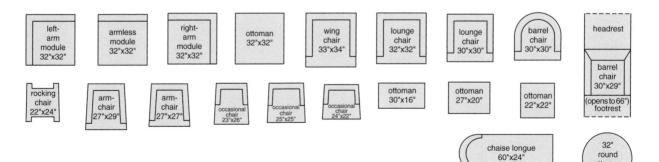

left-arm module 32"x32" · armless module 32"x32" · right-arm module 32"x32" · ottoman 32"x32" · wing chair 33"x34" · lounge chair 32"x32" · lounge chair 30"x30" · barrel chair 30"x30" · headrest

rocking chair 22"x24" · arm-chair 27"x29" · arm-chair 27"x27" · occasional chair 23"x26" · occasional chair 25"x25" · occasional chair 24"x22" · ottoman 30"x16" · ottoman 27"x20" · ottoman 22"x22" · barrel chair 30"x29" (opens to 66") footrest

chaise longue 60"x24" · 32" round ottoman

Furniture Templates

Sofas, Love Seats, and Sofa Beds

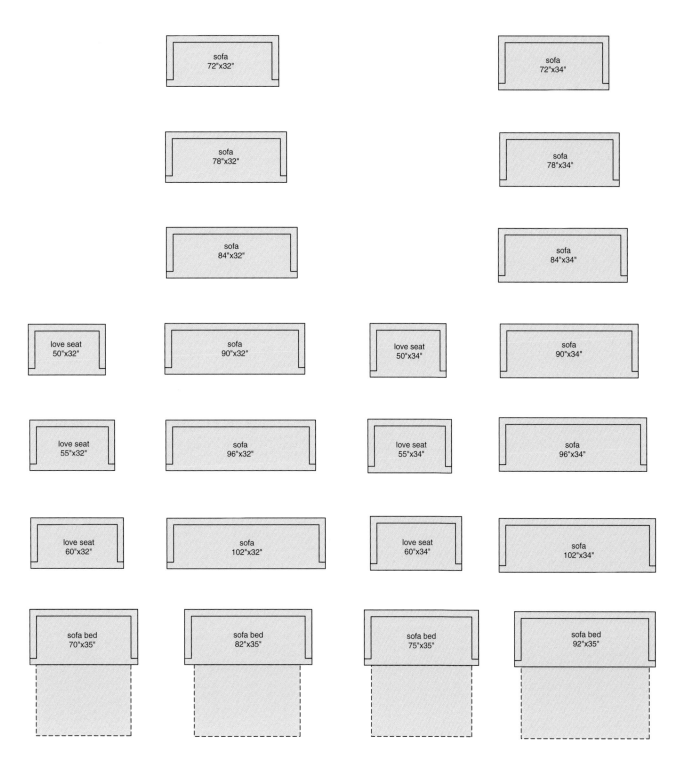

sofa 72"x32"

sofa 72"x34"

sofa 78"x32"

sofa 78"x34"

sofa 84"x32"

sofa 84"x34"

love seat 50"x32"

sofa 90"x32"

love seat 50"x34"

sofa 90"x34"

love seat 55"x32"

sofa 96"x32"

love seat 55"x34"

sofa 96"x34"

love seat 60"x32"

sofa 102"x32"

love seat 60"x34"

sofa 102"x34"

sofa bed 70"x35"

sofa bed 82"x35"

sofa bed 75"x35"

sofa bed 92"x35"

Scale: 1 square=1 foot

resource guide

The following list of manufacturers and associations is meant to be a general guide to additional industry and product-related sources. It is not intended as a listing of products and manufacturers represented by the photographs in this book.

ASSOCIATIONS

American Academy of Pediatrics (AAP)
141 Northwest Point Blvd.
Elk Grove Village, IL 60007
847-434-4000
www.aap.org
A national organization of pediatric health providers with information for parents and a referral service.

American Association of Poison Control Centers (AAPCC)
3201 New Mexico Ave., Ste. 330
Washington, DC 20016
202-362-7217
www.aapcc.org
A national organization that provides listings of local poison-control centers.

American Society of Interior Designers (ASID)
608 Massachusetts Ave., NE
Washington, DC 20002
202-546-3480
www.asid.org
A national organization, with state chapters, that provides a designer referral service to consumers.

American SIDS Institute
509 Augusta Dr.
Marietta, GA 30067
800-232-7437
www.sids.org
A nonprofit organization dedicated to the prevention of sudden infant death syndrome.

Better Sleep Council (BSC)
501 Wythe St.
Alexandria, VA 22314
www.bettersleep.org
Provides related consumer information.

Consumer Product Safety Commission (CPSC)
800-638-2772
www.cpsc.gov
An independent federal regulatory agency that offers information about products and safety recalls.

Home Sewing Association
P. O. Box 1312
Monroeville, PA 15146
412-372-5950
www.sewing.org
Provides project information, press releases, and sewing-related links on its Web site.

International Association for Child Safety (IAFCS)
P. O. Box 801
Summit, NJ 07902
888-677-4227
www.iafcs.com
A nonprofit organization offering safety advice to parents, including referrals to child-safety professionals.

Juvenile Products Manufacturers Association (JPMA)
17000 Commerce Pkwy., Ste. C
Mt. Laurel, NJ 08054
856-638-0420
www.jpma.org
An organization that promotes child-care product safety.

National Safety Council (NSC)
1121 Spring Lake Dr.
Itasca, IL 60143
800-621-7619
www.nsc.org
A nonprofit public service organization.

Window Covering Safety Council
355 Lexington Ave., Ste. 1500
New York, NY 10017
800-506-4636
www.windowcoverings.org
Provides consumers with educational information, including window-cord safety.

MANUFACTURERS & DISTRIBUTORS

Bassett Furniture
3525 Fairystone Park Hwy.
PO Box 626
Bassett, VA 24055
276-629-6000
www.bassettfurniture.com
Manufactures furniture, including juvenile bedroom furniture.

Bébé Sounds
15 W. 36th St., 6th Fl.
New York, NY 10018
800-430-0222
www.bebesounds.com
A division of Unisar, Inc., manufactures the Angel Care Monitor, Movement Sensor, Nursery Air Purifier, and other products.

Benjamin Moore & Co.
www.benjaminmoore.com
Manufactures paint.

Blonder Accents
3950 Prospect Ave.
Cleveland, OH 44115
800-321-4070
www.blonderwall.com
Manufactures wallcoverings and fabrics.

Broyhill Furniture
One Broyhill Park
Lenoir, NC 28633
800-327-6944
www.broyhillfurn.com
Manufactures furniture, including juvenile bedroom furniture.

CoCaLo, Inc.
2920 Red Hill Ave.
Costa Mesa, CA 92626
714-434-7200
www.cocalo.com
Manufactures juvenile bedding under the brand names CoCaLo, Oshkosh B' Gosh, Baby Martex, and Kimberly Grant.

DuPont Stainmaster
800-438-7668
www.dupont.com/stainmaster
Manufactures stain-resistant carpeting.

Enabling Devices
385 Warburton Ave.
Hastings-on-Hudson, NY 10706
800-832-8697
www.enablingdevices.com
Manufactures products and toys for children with special needs.

Finn + Hattie
P. O. Box 539
Yarmouth, ME 04096
207-846-9166
www.finnandhattie.com
Manufactures juvenile furniture.

Ikea
www.ikea.com
Manufactures furniture and accessories, available nationwide.

Kids II
555 North Point Center E., Ste. 600
Alpharetta, GA 30005
770-751-0442
www.kidsii.com
Distributes safety products and toys.

Kolcraft
800-453-7673
www.kolcraft.com
Manufactures juvenile bedding.

Lambs and Ivy
2040-2042 E. Maple Ave.
El Segundo, CA 90245
800-345-2627
www.lambsandivy.com
Manufactures juvenile bedding, rugs, lamps, and accessories.

Let's Learn Educational Toys, Inc.
1 Slater Dr.
Elizabeth, NJ
908-629-9797
www.letslearntoys.com
Manufactures educational toys for children.

Mannington Mills, Inc.
75 Mannington Mills Rd.
Salem, NJ 08079
856-935-3000
www.mannington.com
Manufactures resilient, engineered hardwood, porcelain, and high-pressure plastic laminate flooring.

Motif Designs
20 Jones St.
New Rochelle, NY 10802
www.motif-designs.com
Manufactures furniture, fabrics, and wallcoverings.

PatchKraft
800-866-2229
www.patchkraft.com
Manufactures coordinated bedding for cribs and twin- and full-size beds, using infant-safe fabrics.

Plaid Industries
P. O. Box 7600
Norcross, GA 30091
800-842-4197
www.plaidonline.com
Manufactures stencils, stamps, and craft paints.

Seabrook Wallcoverings, Inc.
1325 Farmville Rd.
Memphis, TN 38122
800-238-9152
www.seabrookwallpaper.com
Manufactures borders and wallcoverings.

Shaw Industries, Inc.
616 E. Walnut Ave.
Dalton, GA 30722
800-441-7429
www.shawinc.com
Manufactures carpet, hardwood, laminate, and porcelain flooring.

Tarkett
www.tarkett-floors.com
Manufactures vinyl, laminate, tile, and wood flooring.

Teragren
12715 Miller Rd.
Bainbridge Island, WA 98110
800-929-6333
www.teragren.com
Manufactures bamboo flooring, panels, and veneers.

TFH USA
4537 Gibsonia Rd.
Gibsonia, PA 15044
800-467-6222
www.tfhusa.com
Manufactures toys and products for children with special needs.

The Well Appointed House
19 E. 65th St., Ste. 7B
New York, NY
888-935-5277
www.wellappointedhouse.com
Sells and distributes juvenile furnishings nationwide.

Thibaut
480 Frelinghuysen Ave.
Newark, NJ 07114
800-223-0704
www.thibautdesign.com
Manufactures wallcovering, borders, and fabric.

Tots in Mind
215 S. Broadway, Ste. 312
Salem, NH 03079
800-626-0339
www.totsinmind.com
Manufactures baby- and toddler-related products.

Waverly
79 Madison Ave.
New York, NY 10016
800-423-5881
www.waverly.com
Manufactures bedding, wallcoverings, and window treatments.

York Wallcoverings
700 Linden Ave.
York, PA 17404
717-846-4456
www.yorkwall.com
Manufactures borders and wallcoverings.

glossary OF KIDS' ROOMS TERMS

Accent lighting: A type of lighting that highlights an area or object to emphasize that aspect of a room's character.

Accessible designs: Products and floor plans that accommodate persons with physical disabilities.

Acrylic paint: A water-soluble paint with a plastic polymer (acrylic) binder.

Adaptable designs: Products and floor plans that can be easily changed or adjusted to accommodate a person with disabilities.

Alkyd paint: A paint-thinner-soluble paint that contains a binder made of soy or urethane resins (alkyds). It is often imprecisely called "oil-based" paint. Alkyds have replaced linseed oil, which was used as a binder in oil-based paint.

Analogous scheme: See *Harmonious Color Scheme*.

Ambient lighting: General or background illumination that surrounds a room, such as the light produced by a ceiling fixture or cove lighting.

Armoire: A large, often ornate cupboard or wardrobe used for storage.

Backlight: Illumination coming from a source behind or adjacent to an object.

Blender brushes: Specialty brushes used to blend and soften all types of wet painted surfaces.

Box pleat: A double pleat, underneath which the edges fold toward each other.

Broadloom: A wide loom for weaving carpeting that is 54 inches wide or more.

Built-in: A permanent element, such as a bookcase or cabinetry, that is built into a wall or an existing frame.

Case goods: Furniture used for storage, including cabinets, dressers, and desks.

Chaise longue: A chair with back support and a seat long enough for outstretched legs.

Cheesecloth: A loosely woven, coarse cotton gauze used to create different textures as well as to blend and smooth wet paint over a surface.

Clear topcoat: A transparent finishing layer of protection applied over a decorated surface.

Clearance: The amount of space between two fixtures, the centerlines of two fixtures, or a fixture and an obstacle, such as a wall. Clearances may be mandated by codes.

Code: A locally or nationally enforced mandate regarding structural design, materials, plumbing, or electrical systems that state what you can or cannot do when you build or remodel. Codes are intended to protect standards of health, safety, and land use.

Color scheme: A group of colors used together to create visual harmony in a space.

Color washing: The technique of applying layers of heavily thinned glaze to a surface to produce a faded, transparent wash of color.

Color wheel: A pie-shaped diagram showing the range and relationships of pigment and dye colors. Three equidistant wedge-shaped slices are the primaries; in between are the secondary and tertiary colors into which the primaries combine. Though represented as discrete slices, the hues form a continuum.

Combing: A technique that involves dragging a plastic or metal comb through wet paint or glaze in order to simulate texture or to create a pattern.

Complementary colors: Hues directly opposite each other on the color wheel. As the strongest contrasts, complements tend to intensify each other. A color can be grayed by mixing it with its complement.

Contemporary design: Current or recent design.

Contrast: The art of assembling colors with different values and intensities, and in different proportions, to create a dynamic scheme.

Cornice: A projecting, decorative box installed above a window, designed to cover a curtain rod.

Daybed: A bed made up to appear as a sofa. It usually has a frame that consists of a headboard, a footboard, and a sideboard along the back.

Decoupage: The technique of applying cut-out paper or fabric motifs to a surface, and then coating the images with varnish or decoupage medium.

Decoupage medium: A smooth and glossy glue-like liquid used to apply cut-out paper or fabric images to a surface or an object. It is used as both an adhesive and a top coat.

Dimmer switch: A switch that can vary the intensity of the light it controls.

Distressed finish: A decorative paint technique in which the final paint coat is sanded and battered to produce an aged appearance.

Dovetail: A joinery method in which wedge-shape parts are interlocked to form a tight bond. This joint is commonly used on furniture parts, such as drawers.

Dowel: A short cylinder, made of wood, metal, or plastic, that fits into corresponding holes bored in two pieces of wood, creating a joint.

Dragging: A technique that involves pulling a special long-bristled brush through wet paint or glaze to create fine lines or narrow stripes.

Etagère: Freestanding or hanging shelves for displaying small objects.

Faux: The French word for "false." With regard to painted finishes, it is used to describe any technique in which paint is manipulated on a surface to imitate the appearance of another substance, such as wood or stone.

Flat finish: The absence of sheen after a paint or topcoat dries.

Fluorescent lighting: A glass tube coated on the interior with phosphor, a chemical compound that emits light when activated by ultraviolet energy. Air in the tube is replaced with a combination of argon gas and a small amount of mercury. Lamps are also circular and bulb shaped.

Focal point: The dominant element in a room or design, usually the first to catch your eye.

Frieze: A horizontal band at the top of the wall or just below the cornice.

Glaze: A thinned-down, translucent emulsion that may or may

not contain pigment (color).

Glossy finish: The appearance of sheen after a paint or topcoat dries.

Graining comb: A flexible steel or plastic device with random-size tines or teeth. It is dragged through wet glaze or paint to create striated or grained surfaces. A common hair comb makes a workable substitute.

Ground-fault circuit interrupter (GFCI): A safety circuit breaker that compares the amount of current entering a receptacle with the amount leaving. If there is a discrepancy of 0.005 volt, the GFCI breaks the circuit in a fraction of a second. GFCIs are required by the National Electrical Code in kitchens, bathrooms, laundries—and in any other rooms with plumbing.

Hardware: Wood, plastic, or metal-plated trim found on the exterior of furniture, such as knobs, handles, and decorative trim.

Harmonious color scheme: Also called analogous, a combination focused on neighboring hues on the color wheel. The shared underlying color generally gives such schemes a coherent flow.

Hue: Another term for specific points on the pure, clear range of the color wheel.

Incandescent lighting: A bulb (lamp) that converts electric power into light by passing electric current through a filament of tungsten wire.

Indirect lighting: A more subdued type of lighting that is not head-on, but rather reflected against another surface such as a ceiling.

Lambrequin: A painted board or stiffened fabric that surrounds the top and side of a window in the manner of a valance. Historically, it is drapery that hangs from a shelf (such as a mantel) or the top of a window.

Laminate: One or more thin layers of durable plastic that is bonded to a fabric or a material. It may be used to fabricate furniture, countertops, or flooring.

Latex paint: Paint that contains either acrylic or vinyl resins or a combination of the two. High-quality latex paints contain 100-percent acrylic resin. Latex paint is water-soluble and dries quickly.

Lining brush: A thin, flexible, long-bristled brush used for fine lining and detail work.

Love seat: A sofa-like piece of furniture with seating for two.

Modular: Units of a standard size that can be fitted together in a number of ways.

Molding: An architectural band that can either trim a line where materials join or create a linear decoration. It is typically made of wood, but metal, plaster, or polymer (plastic) is also used.

Mortise-and-tenon joinery: A hole (mortise) cut into a piece of wood that receives a projecting piece (tenon) to create a joint.

Orientation: The placement of any object or space, such as a window, a door, or a room, and its relationship to the points on a compass.

Overglaze: A thin glaze added as a final step to a decorative paint finish. It can be a thinner version of the base coat or it can be mixed in a different color.

Panel: A flat, rectangular piece of material that forms part of a wall, door, or cabinet. Typically made of wood, it is usually framed by a border and either raised or recessed.

Parquet: Inlaid woodwork arranged to form a geometric pattern on a floor. It consists of small blocks of hardwood, which are often stained in contrasting colors.

Pattern matching: To align a repeating pattern when joining together two pieces of fabric or wallpaper.

Polyurethane: A tough, hard-wearing coating made of synthetic resins. It serves as a good top coat or finish on wood cabinets and furniture and can be applied over most types of paint, except artist's oils.

Primary colors: Red, blue, and yellow, which, in pigments, cannot be produced by mixing other colors. Primaries plus black and white, in turn, combine to make all the other hues.

Primers: Primers prepare surfaces for painting by making them more uniform in texture and giving them "tooth."

Sea sponge: A natural sponge, not to be confused with the cellulose variety used in households. It is used to apply paint in a technique called sponging.

Sealers: These products are applied to porous surfaces before painting in order to form a durable, nonabsorbent barrier between the surface and the paint. This avoids a rough, uneven, dull finish.

Secondary color: A mix of two primaries. The secondary colors are orange, green, and purple.

Semigloss: A hard, slightly glossy paint finish or topcoat that is light reflective, somewhere between gloss and eggshell.

Shade: A color to which black or gray has been added to make it darker.

Sheen: The quality of paint that reflects light when it is dry.

Slipcover: A fabric or plastic cover that can be draped or tailored to fit over a piece of furniture.

Spattering: Applying random dots of paint over a surface by striking a saturated brush or by rubbing paint through a screen.

Sponging: A paint technique that involves using a sponge to apply or take off paint.

Stencil: A cutout pattern.

Stenciling: Creating an image or a motif, often in a repeated pattern, by painting a cutout pattern.

Task lighting: Illumination that is focused for performing a specific task, such as reading or grooming.

Thinner: A liquid that is mixed with paint to make it less thick. Mineral spirits may be used for alkyd paints and water for latex paint.

Tint: A color to which white or light gray has been added to make it lighter.

Tone: Degree of lightness or darkness of a color. A color to which gray has been added to change its value.

Tongue-and-groove joinery: A wood joinery technique in which a protruding end (tongue) or edge locks into a recess (groove).

Track lighting: Lighting that utilizes a fixed band that supplies a current to movable light fixtures.

Trompe l'oeil: Literally meaning "fool the eye," a painted mural in which realistic images and the illusion of more space are created. Also, a painted surface that convincingly mimics reality.

Turning: Wood that is cut on a lathe into a round object with a distinctive profile. Furniture legs, posts, rungs, and the like are usually made in this way.

Uplight: Also used to describe the lights themselves, this is actually the term for light that is directed upward toward the ceiling or the upper part of walls.

Valance: A short length of drapery that hangs along the top part of a window, with or without a curtain underneath.

Value: In relation to a scale of grays ranging from black to white, this is the term to describe the lightness (tint) or darkness (shade) of a color.

Veneer: High-quality wood that is cut into very thin sheets for use as a surface material.

Welt: A cord, often covered by fabric, that is used as an edge trimming on cushions and slipcovers.

index

photo credits

Page 1: Mark Lohman, design: Janet Lohman Interior Design **page 2:** Mark Lohman, design: Jeanette Kyser **pages 6–7:** *both* Mark Lohman **page 8:** Eric Roth, design: Susan Sargent **page 10:** Mark Lohman **page 11:** Eric Roth **pages 12–17:** *all* Tony Giammarino/Giammarino & Dworkin, design: Karen Adams **page 18–23:** *all* Mark Samu, architect: EJR Architecture **pages 24–25:** *both* Beth Singer **pages 26–27:** *both* Mark Samu, design: Correia Design **pages 28–29:** *all* Mark Samu, builder: Amedore Homes, Inc., courtesy of Builder/Architect Magazine **pages 30–31:** *all* Mark Samu, design: Correia Design **page 32:** Tony Giammarino/Giammarino & Dworkin, design: Cheryl Palmore **page 34:** *left* Tony Giammarino/Giammarino & Dworkin, painter: Beth Scherr; *right* Tony Giammarino/Giammarino & Dworkin, design: Alison Monroe **page 35:** *both* Tony Giammarino/Giammarino & Dworkin, design: Karen Adams **page 38:** Mark Samu, design: Correia Design **page 39:** Olson Photographic, LLC, design: Infant Interiors **page 40:** Tria Giovan **page 41:** Mark Samu, design: Artistic Design by Deidre **pages 42–43:** *both* Tria Giovan **page 44:** Bob Greenspan, stylist: Susan Andrews **pages 46–47:** *all* Tony Giammarino/Giammarino & Dworkin, design: Pat Stockdon **pages 48–49:** *all* Tony Giammarino/Giammarino & Dworkin **page 50:** Olson Photographic, LLC **page 52:** Tony Giammarino/Giammarino & Dworkin **page 53:** *both* Mark Samu, builder: Manchester Associates, LTD., courtesy of Builder/Architect Magazine **pages 54:** Brian Vanden Brink, architect: Nancy Barba **page 55:** Brian Vanden Brink, architect: Tom Catalano **page 56:** *top left* david-duncanlivingston.com; *top right* Tria Giovan, design: Jennifer Garrigue; *bottom* Mark Lohman **page 57:** Bob Greenspan, stylist: Susan Andrews **pages 58–59:** *top* Olson Photographic, LLC;

bottom Olson Photographic, LLC, design: Lisa Newman **page 60:** *both* courtesy of Finn + Hattie **page 61:** Olson Photographic, LLC **page 62:** Brian Vanden Brink, architect: Polhemus Savery DaSilva **page 63:** *left* Tony Giammarino/Giammarino & Dworkin, design: Pat Stockdon; *right* Mark Samu/CH **page 64:** *left* Tria Giovan; *right* Mark Lohman, design: Janet Lohman Interior Design **page 65:** Karyn R. Millet, design: Bonesteel Trout Hall **page 66:** Mark Lohman **page 67:** Olson Photographic, LLC, design: Autore Interiors **pages 68–69:** *left* Minh + Wass; *center* Eric Roth, design: Marchella's; *right* Greg Hursley **page 70:** Alun Callender/Redcover.com **page 71:** Mark Lohman, design: Janet Lohman Interior Design **pages 72–73:** *all* Olson Photographic, LLC **pages 74–75:** *all* Bob Greenspan, stylist: Susan Andrews **page 76:** Mark Lohman, design: Jeanette Kyser **page 78:** Johnny Bouchier/Redcover.com **page 79:** *top* Eric Roth, design: Susan Sargent; *bottom* Johnny Bouchier/Redcover.com **page 80:** Tony Giammarino/Giammarino & Dworkin, design: Karen Adams **page 81:** Brian Vanden Brink **page 82:** *top* Tony Giammarino/Giammarino & Dworkin, design: Karen Adams; *bottom* david-duncanlivingston.com **page 83:** Eric Roth **page 84:** Mark Lohman, design Kathryne Designs **page 85:** *top* Mark Lohman; *bottom* Brad Simmons **page 86:** *top* Mark Lohman, design: Jeanette Kyser; *bottom* Beth Singer, design: Kris Appleby and Kay Ponticall/Detroit Suite Dreams Showhouse, artist: Bill Bradley **page 87:** *top* Mark Lohman, design: Lizzie McGraw; *bottom left* Mark Lohman; *bottom right* Mark Lohman, design: Sally Dixon **page 88:** Minh + Wass **page 89:** Mark Lohman, design: Jeanette Kyser **pages 90–91:** *left* Olson Photographic, LLC; *center* Eric Roth, architect: Benjamin Nutter; *right* courtesy of Teragren **page 92:** courtesy of Mannington

page 93: courtesy of Tarkett **page 95:** Tony Giammarino/Giammarino & Dworkin, design: Karen Adams **page 96:** *top* Tony Giammarino/Giammarino & Dworkin, design: Karen Adams; *bottom* courtesy of Shaw **page 97:** Tony Giammarino/Giammarino & Dworkin, design: Karen Adams **pages 98–99:** *all* Eric Roth **page 100:** Eric Roth, design: Pamela Copeman **pages 102–103:** *all* Karyn R. Millet, design: Elizabeth Dinkel Design Associates **page 105:** *both* Eric Roth **page 106:** Mark Samu, design: Correia Design **page 107:** Tony Giammarino/Giammarino & Dworkin, design: Pat Stockdon **pages 108–109:** *both* Mark Samu, design: Pascucci/Delisle Design **page 110:** Eric Roth **page 111:** Mark Lohman **pages 112–113:** *both* Eric Roth **pages 114–115:** *all* Olson Photographic, LLC, design: Infant Interiors **pages 116–117:** *all* Mark Samu **page 118:** Mark Lohman, design: Lizzie McGraw **page 120:** *left* Mark Lohman; *right* Tony Giammarino/Giammarino & Dworkin **page 121:** Lucinda Symons/Redcover.com **pages 122–123:** *left & bottom right* Redcover.com; *top right* Ed Reeve/Redcover.com **page 124:** *both* Redcover.com **page 125:** Wesley Rose **page 126:** Tony Giammarino/Giammarino & Dworkin **pages 127–128:** *both* Lucinda Symons/Redcover.com **page 129:** Mark Lohman **page 130:** Tony Giammarino/Giammarino & Dworkin **page 132:** Tony Giammarino/Giammarino & Dworkin, painter: Elizabeth Arnold **page 134:** *top* Olson Photographic, LLC; *bottom both* Mark Lohman, design: Sue McKeehan **page 135:** Mark Lohman, design: Sue McKeehan **page 136:** *top* Mark Lohman; *bottom* Tony Giammarino/Giammarino & Dworkin **page 137:** Brian Vanden Brink, builder: Boothbay Homebuilders **page 138:** Tria Giovan, design: Suzanne Kalser **pages 141:** Mark Lohman, design: Jeanette Kyser **page 142:** *right & bottom left* Mark Lohman, design: Sally Dixon;

top left Mark Lohman **page 143:** Mark Lohman, design: Jeanette Kyser **page 144:** *top* Tria Giovan; *bottom* Mark Lohman **page 145:** Mark Lohman, design: Kitty Bartholomew **page 146:** Mark Samu, builder: The Michaels Group, courtesy of Builder/Architect Magazine **page 147:** Tria Giovan **page 148:** Eric Roth, design: Kelly McGuill/Americana Designs **page 149:** *top* Tria Giovan, design: Lynn Morgan; *bottom* Mark Lohman **page 150:** Eric Roth, architect: Morse Constructions **page 151:** Tria Giovan, design: Bill Stern **page 152:** Mark Lohman, design: Janet Lohman Interior Design **page 153:** Eric Roth **pages 154–155:** *all* Mark Samu, builder: Manchester Associates, LTD., courtesy of Builder/Architect Magazine **pages 156–157:** *all* Eric Roth **page 158:** Mark Lohman, design: Jan Dutcher **page 160:** Tria Giovan **page 161:** Eric Roth, design: Frank Roop **page 162:** Mark Lohman, design: Jan Dutcher **page 164:** Tony Giammarino/Giammarino & Dworkin, design: Susan Eckis **page 165:** Tria Giovan **pages 166–167:** *both* Mark Lohman **pages 168–169:** *all* courtesy of KooKoo Bear Kids **page 170:** Mark Samu, architect: EJR Architecture **page 171:** Mark Lohman, design: Andy Marcus **page 172:** david-duncanlivingston.com **page 173:** *top right* Mark Samu, architect: EJR Architecture; *bottom* Jessie Walker; *top left* Tony Giammarino/Giammarino & Dworkin **page 174:** Olson Photographic, LLC, design: J Interiors **page 175:** Mark Samu, builder: Amedore homes, Inc., courtesy of Builder/Architect Magazine **pages 176–177:** *all* Mark Lohman **pages 178–179:** *all* Tria Giovan **page 180:** Lucinda Symons/Redcover.com **page 182:** Eric Roth **page 183:** Olson Photographic, LLC **page 184:** Tria Giovan **page 185:** Mark Samu, design: Correia Design **page 186:** Mark Lohman, design: Sue McKeehan **page 187:** *top* Olson Photographic, LLC; *bottom* Mark Samu,

design: Correia Design **page 189:** Eric Roth **pages 190–191:** *all* Jake Fitzjones/Redcover.com **page 192:** Mark Lohman, design: Janet Lohman Interior Design **page 194:** Eric Roth **page 195:** Olson Photographic, LLC, design: Ambiente/Venlo **page 196:** Mark Lohman, design: Janet Lohman Interior Design **page 197:** Eric Roth **page 198:** Olson Photographic, LLC, design: J Interiors **page 199:** Casey Dunn **page 200:** *both* Eric Roth

page 201: Anne Gummerson **page 211:** Johnny Bouchier/Redcover.com **page 212:** Tony Giammarino/Giammarino & Dworkin, design: Pat Stockdon **page 213:** Tony Giammarino/Giammarino & Dworkin **page 214:** Bob Greenspan, stylist: Susan Andrews **pages 215–216:** *both* Mark Samu **page 217:** Olson Photographic, LLC **page 223:** Mark Lohman

If you like
The Smart Approach to® Kids' Rooms
take a look at our other Smart Approach books

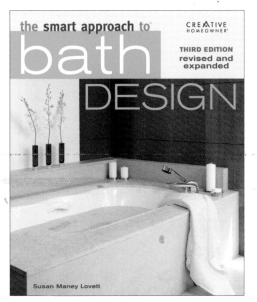
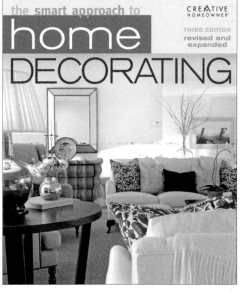
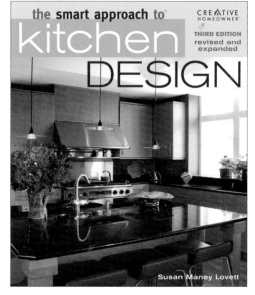
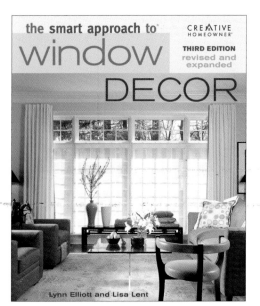
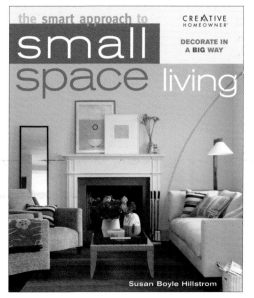
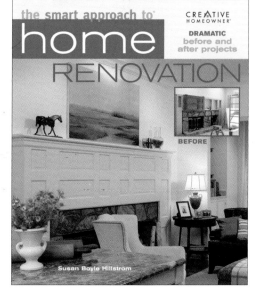